The Heroine's Journey

Books by Maureen Murdock

The Heroine's Journey: Woman's Quest for Wholeness

*Spinning Inward: Using Guided Imagery with Children for
Learning, Creativity, and Relaxation*

THE HEROINE'S JOURNEY

Maureen Murdock

Shambhala
Boulder
1990

Shambhala Publications, Inc.
4720 Walnut Street
Boulder, Colorado 80301
www.shambhala.com

22   21   20   19   18   17

Printed in the United States of America
∞ This edition is printed on acid-free paper that meets
the American National Standards Institute Z39.48 Standard.

♻ Shambhala Publications makes every effort to print on recycled paper.
For more information please visit www.shambhala.com.

Distributed in the United States by Penguin Random House LLC
and in Canada by Random House of Canada Ltd

Library of Congress Cataloging-in-Publication Data

Murdock, Maureen.
The heroine's journey/
Maureen Murdock—1st ed.
p. cm.
ISBN 978-0-87773-485-7 (alk. paper)
1. Women—Psychology.   2. Femininity
(Psychology).   3. Sex role.
I. Title.
HQ1206.M85   1990   89-43513
305.42—dc20   CIP

*To my mother and
my daughter*

Contents

Acknowledgments

The Heroine's Journey is the work of many women with whom I have cojourneyed. I'd like to express my appreciation in particular to the women in my women's groups over the past twelve years. We have gone through all the stages of the journey together, functioning as allies, ogres, co-wanderers, healers, and finally becoming a cackling council of crones.

I learned about the subtle differences between the male and female quest from the participants in my workshops and classes on the hero/heroine's journey. My thanks in particular to those men and women whose quest it was to heal their feminine wound. I am grateful for the opportunity to have shared the journeys of the women I led on vision quest, women in therapy, my women friends, and the women in my family. I am especially grateful to those women who have generously allowed me to retell their dreams and stories in this book.

One woman in particular has been my guide in allowing me to release my reliance on the old heroic model and in helping me heal my own mother/daughter split: to Gilda Frantz I offer my deepest thanks for being there and for encouraging the process of my creative journey.

My thanks to the people whom I interviewed during the preparation of this book: to Joseph Campbell who was there at the beginning and to the women artists and poets whose work deeply expresses their commitment to reclaiming the power and beauty of the feminine. Thanks also to the Impossible Women group with whom I first shared my diagram of the heroine's journey.

Several people have assisted me in preparing this manuscript: my daughter, Heather, who functioned as my assistant with research, footnotes, editing, and general good cheer; Jeffrey Herring, who tracked down permissions; and my husband, Lucien Wulsin, my Man with Heart, who has always encouraged my journey and has been there as fair witness to my descents. The staff at the Jung Library in Los Angeles have given of their time and assistance generously, and Martha Walford has shared her slides of ancient goddess artifacts, while Sandra Stafford has drawn the illustrations.

I am especially grateful to my editor, Emily Hilburn Sell, at Shambhala Publications, with whom I shared many laughs during the final preparation of this book. I appreciated her humor, down-to-earth wisdom, and initial enthusiasm about this project. I'd like to acknowledge the spiritual assistance I have consistently received from the Great Mother during the unraveling of this heroine's quest. Her image sits on my computer in many guises: my thanks to Mother Bear, Kwan Yin, Mari-Aphrodite, Nut, and Mahuea. Finally, thanks to the women of my woman line for their Celtic strength, songs, storytelling, and devotion to the unseen realms.

The Heroine's Journey

Introduction

There is a void felt these days by women and men—who
suspect that their feminine nature, like Persephone, has
gone to hell. Wherever there is such a void, such a gap or
wound agape, healing must be sought in the blood of the
wound itself. It is another of the old alchemical truths
that "no solution should be made except in its own
blood." So the female void cannot be cured by conjunction with the male, but rather by an internal conjunction,
by an integration of its own parts, by a remembering or a
putting back together of the mother-daughter body.
                              Nor Hall, *The Moon and the Virgin*

Working as a therapist with women, particularly between the
ages of thirty and fifty, I have heard a resounding cry of
dissatisfaction with the successes won in the marketplace. This
dissatisfaction is described as a sense of sterility, emptiness,
and dismemberment, even a sense of betrayal. These women
have embraced the stereotypical male heroic journey and have
attained academic, artistic, or financial success; yet for many
the question remains, "What is all of this for?"

The boon of success leaves these women overscheduled,
exhausted, suffering from stress-related ailments, and wonder-
ing how they got off-track. This was not what they had
bargained for when they first pursued achievement and recognition. The image they held of the view from the top did not
include sacrifice of body and soul. In noticing the physical
and emotional damage incurred by women on this heroic
quest, I have concluded that the reason they are experiencing

so much pain is that they chose to follow a model that denies who they are.

My desire to understand how the woman's journey relates to the journey of the hero first led me to talk with Joseph Campbell in 1981. I knew that the stages of the heroine's journey incorporated aspects of the journey of the hero, but I felt that the focus of female spiritual development was to heal the internal split between woman and her feminine nature. I wanted to hear Campbell's views. I was surprised when he responded that women don't need to make the journey. "In the whole mythological tradition the woman is *there*. All she has to do is to realize that she's the place that people are trying to get to. When a woman realizes what her wonderful character is, she's not going to get messed up with the notion of being pseudo-male."[1]

This answer stunned me; I found it deeply unsatisfying. The women I know and work with do not want to be *there*, the place that people are trying to get to. They do not want to embody Penelope, waiting patiently, endlessly weaving and unweaving. They do not want to be handmaidens of the dominant male culture, giving service to the gods. They do not want to follow the advice of fundamentalist preachers and return to the home. They need a new model that understands who and what a woman is. In *Daybook: The Journal of an Artist* Anne Truitt writes:

> The cave of womanhood feels cozy to me, and I shall always, I think, retreat to it with the comfortable feeling that I am where I should be in some sense deeper than words can articulate. So men may feel about some cave of manhood that I can only imagine. There is sturdy common sense in accepting the differences between men and women as salt. But because womanhood is "home" to me does not mean that I wish to stay home all the time. The cave would become fetid if I never went out. I have too much energy, too much curiosity, too much force to remain so confined. Whole areas of myself would either atrophy or sour. If I wish to be responsible to myself, and I do, I have to pursue my aspirations.[2]

Women do have a quest at this time in our culture. It is the quest to fully embrace their feminine nature, learning how to value themselves as women and to heal the deep wound of the feminine. It is a very important inner journey toward being a fully integrated, balanced, and whole human being. Like most journeys, the path of the heroine is not easy; it has no well-defined guideposts nor recognizable tour guides. There is no map, no navigational chart, no chronological age when the journey begins. It follows no straight lines. It is a journey that seldom receives validation from the outside world; in fact the outer world often sabotages and interferes with it.

The model of the heroine's journey is derived in part from Campbell's model of the heroic quest.[3] The language of the stages, however, is particular to women, and the visual model appeared to me in a very feminine way. It emerged out of my back.

In spring 1983 I was in a postgraduate training program at the Los Angeles Family Institute studying a therapeutic technique called "family sculpting." Family sculpting uses enactment of a scene repeated in a person's family of origin, such as a typical dinner scenario. I was participating as myself in a dinner scene that included my mother, father, and younger sister, whose roles were played by fellow students. As we held the frozen positions once held by my family members, my back went out. I could no longer sustain the position I had held of "bending over backwards" to keep the peace.

I was immobilized for three days. I lay on the living room floor on my stomach and cried about the pain and chaos in my family that I had learned to shut out through work and overachievement. Out of those tears came the image of the heroine's journey, a circular path that moved clockwise. It began with a very abrupt rejection of the feminine as defined by me as dependent, overcontrolling, and full of rage. It continued with total submersion into the familiar outer heroic journey, complete with masculine allies, to achieve the boon of independence, prestige, money, power, and success. This was followed by a bewildering period of dryness and despair which led to an inevitable descent to the underworld to meet the *dark feminine*.

Out of this darkness came an urgent need to heal what I call the *mother/daughter split*, the *deep feminine wound*. The return trip involved a redefinition and validation of feminine values and an integration of these with the masculine skills learned during the first half of the journey.

The image appeared whole as it is shown on page 5, and it has been my task in the intervening years to understand the stages of the journey. This has been a slow process of listening to the stories of my clients and friends and looking at the deeper level of my own need for recognition and approval in a male-dominated society.

This journey is described from my perspective and from the perspective of many of the women of my generation who have sought validation from patriarchal systems and found them not only lacking but terribly destructive. We are the children of the post-Sputnik era who were encouraged to excel in order to recover Western supremacy.

I am what is called a *father's daughter*—a woman who has identified primarily with the father, often rejecting the mother, and who has sought attention and approval from the father and masculine values. The model I am presenting does not necessarily fit the experience of all women of all ages, and I have found that neither is it limited only to women. It addresses the journeys of both genders. It describes the experience of many people who strive to be active and make a contribution in the world, but who also fear what our progress-oriented society has done to the human psyche and to the ecological balance of the planet.

Movement through the stages of the journey is cyclic, and a person may be at several stages of the journey at one time. For example, I am working on healing my mother/daughter split as well as integrating the two parts of my nature. The heroine's journey is a continuous cycle of development, growth, and learning.

The journey begins with our heroine's search for identity. This "call" is heard at no specific age but occurs when the "old

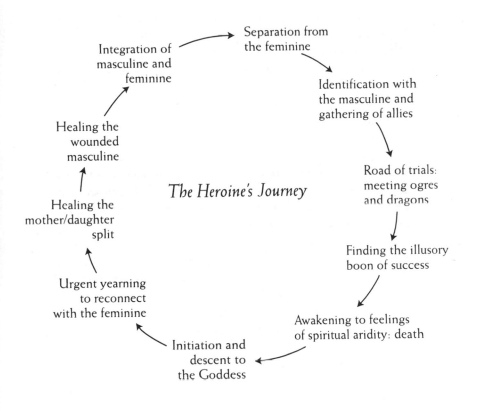

The Heroine's Journey

- Separation from the feminine
- Identification with the masculine and gathering of allies
- Road of trials: meeting ogres and dragons
- Finding the illusory boon of success
- Awakening to feelings of spiritual aridity: death
- Initiation and descent to the Goddess
- Urgent yearning to reconnect with the feminine
- Healing the mother/daughter split
- Healing the wounded masculine
- Integration of masculine and feminine

The heroine's journey begins with "Separation from the feminine" and ends with "Integration of masculine and feminine."

self" no longer fits. This may be when the young woman leaves home for college, work, travel, or relationship. Or it may be when a woman in mid-life divorces, returns to work or school, changes career, or is faced with an empty nest. Or it may simply occur when a woman realizes that she has no sense of self that she can call her own.

This beginning stage of the journey often includes a rejection of the feminine as defined as passive, manipulative, or nonproductive. Women have often been portrayed in our society as unfocused, fickle, and too emotional to get the job done. This lack of focus and clear differentiation in women is perceived as weak, inferior, and dependent—not only by the dominant culture but by many women as well.

Women who seek success in the male-oriented work world often choose this path to dispel that myth. They seek to prove that they have good minds, can follow through, and are both emotionally and financially independent. They discuss issues with their fathers and male relatives. They choose role models and mentors who are men or male-identified women and who validate their intellect, sense of purpose, and ambition and generate a sense of security, direction, and success. Everything is geared to getting the job done; climbing the academic or corporate ladder; achieving prestige, position, and financial equity; and feeling powerful in the world. This is a heady experience for the heroine, and it is fully supported by our materialistic society, which places supreme value on what you *do*. Anything less than doing "important work in the world" has no intrinsic value.

Our heroine puts on her armor, picks up her sword, chooses her swiftest steed, and goes into battle. She finds her treasure: an advanced degree, a corporate title, money, authority. The men smile, shake her hand, and welcome her to the club.

After a period of time of enjoying the view from the top, managing it all, including perhaps both career *and* kids, there may be a feeling of "Okay, I've arrived; what's next?" She looks for the next hurdle to jump, the next promotion, the next social event, filling every spare moment with *doing*. She doesn't know how to stop or say no and feels guilty at the idea of disappointing anyone who needs her. Achieving has become an addiction, and there is an incredible "high" associated with her newly won power.

It is often at this stage that a woman begins to feel out of sync with herself, or she may experience a physical illness or accident. She begins to ask, "What is all of this for? I've achieved everything I've set out to achieve and I feel empty. Why do I have this gnawing sensation of loneliness and desolation? Why this sense of betrayal? What have I lost?"

In her desire to dispel the negative associations with the feminine, our heroine has created an imbalance within herself which has left her scarred and broken. She has learned how to get things done logically and efficiently but has sacrificed her health, dreams, and intuition. What she may have lost is a deep relationship to her own feminine nature. She may describe and mourn the numbing of her body wisdom, the lack of time for family or creative projects, the loss of deep friendships with other women, or the absence of her own "little girl."

According to Campbell, "woman is primarily concerned with fostering. She can foster a body, foster a soul, foster a civilization, foster a community. If she has nothing to foster, she somehow loses the sense of her function."[1] I find that many women who have embraced the masculine hero's journey have forgotten how to foster—themselves. They have assumed that to be successful they have to keep their edges sharp, and in that process many have ended up with a hole in their hearts.

What Campbell says of men in their mid-life crisis may also apply to the perplexity and dissatisfaction women feel in the face of success. "They've gotten to the top of the ladder and found it's against the wrong wall. They made some misjudgments in the beginning."[5]

Some women find that their strivings for success and recognition have been predicated on pleasing parents, particularly the internalized father. When they begin to look at their motivation, some have a hard time finding the parts of themselves that are their own. A feeling of desolation takes hold. "When I look inside, I don't know who's there," says a filmmaker in her early forties. "The only thing I am sure of is a yearning to whole my heart. The only thing I can trust is my body."

What has happened to these women is that they didn't travel far enough on the road to liberation. They learned how to be successful according to a masculine model, but that model did not satisfy the need to be a whole person. The "misjudgment in the beginning" may have been a decision to play by others' rules for self-worth and success. When a woman decides not to play by patriarchal rules anymore, she has no guidelines telling her how to act or how to feel. When she no longer wants to perpetuate archaic forms, life becomes exciting—and terrifying. "Change is frightening but where there's fear, there's power. If we learn to feel our fear without letting it stop us, fear can become an ally, a sign to tell us that something we have encountered can be transformed. Often our true strength is not in the things that represent what is familiar, comfortable, or positive but in our fear and even in our resistance to change."[6] An initiation process has begun.

During this part of the journey, the woman begins her descent. It may involve a seemingly endless period of wandering, grief, and rage; of dethroning kings; of looking for the lost pieces of herself and meeting the dark feminine. It may take weeks, months, or years, and for many it may involve a time of voluntary isolation—a period of darkness and silence and of learning the art of deeply listening once again to self: of *being* instead of doing. The outer world may see this as a depression and a period of stasis. Family, friends, and work associates implore our heroine to "get on with it."

This period is often filled with dreams of dismemberment and death, of shadow sisters and intruders, of journeys across deserts and rivers, of ancient goddess symbols and sacred animals. There is a desire to spend more time in nature being nurtured by the earth and an increasing awareness of seasonal changes and the rhythms of the moon. For many women, the time of menstruation becomes an important occasion to honor womanhood, blood, the cleansing and renewal of body and soul. The descent cannot be hurried because it is a sacred journey, one not only of reclaiming the lost parts of oneself, but also of rediscovering the lost soul of the culture—what many women today view as reclaiming the Goddess. An entry from my own journal during this period reads:

"This is uncharted territory. It's dark, moist, bloody, and lonely. I see no allies, no comfort, no signs out. I feel scraped open and raw. I look for the dismembered parts of myself— something recognizable—but there are only fragments and I don't know how to put them together. This is unlike any struggle I've had before. It's not the conquest of the other; it's coming face to face with myself. I walk naked looking for the Mother. Looking to reclaim the parts of myself that have not seen the light of day. They must be here in the darkness. They wait for me to find them because they no longer trust. I have disowned them before. They are my treasures but I have to dig for them. This journey is not about some fairy god-mother showing me the way out. I dig . . . for patience, for the courage to endure the dark, for the perserverance not to rise to the light prematurely, cutting short my meeting with the Mother."

After the period of descent our heroine begins to slowly heal the mother/daughter split, the wound that occurred with the initial rejection of the feminine. This may or may not involve an actual healing of the relationship between a woman and her own mother. A healing does occur, however, within the woman herself as she begins to nurture her body and soul and reclaim her feelings, intuition, sexuality, creativity, and humor.

There may be a sudden urge to take a ceramics or cooking class, to garden, to be massaged, to create a comfortable nest. Some of the energy that has been outer-directed is slowly redirected to giving birth to creative projects, rediscovering the body, and enjoying the company of other women. Women whose primary focus has been career-oriented may now seek marriage and child-bearing. This stage involves clear choices and sacrifices that to anyone with a patriarchal focus may look like dropping out.

A client of mine, a dentist in her late thirties who had

already lost one breast to cancer, decided to write, garden, and to mother. "It is a difficult decision; the steady paycheck makes me feel secure and useful, and I expect that it will be close to impossible to get health insurance because of my pre-existing condition. But I'm impatient to be doing those things that were important to me before dentistry pushed everything aside."

I had a similar experience while writing this book. The outer journey for recognition became less and less important as I explored the inner terrain. My feminine voice became stronger as I developed the courage to let go of my reliance on linear mind. Then I was free to listen to dreams, images, and inner allies. These became my guides. When a woman reduces the emphasis on the outer heroic quest for self-definition, she is free to explore *her* images and *her* voice.

As a woman focuses on the process of the inner journey, she receives little recognition and less applause from the outer world. The questions she asks about life values make those who are committed to the quest for the outer trappings of success uncomfortable. This is why such a journey involves courage and trust that spiritual assistance will be provided. Women are coming together to study, to share images, and to honor what is feminine and what has been lost to themselves and to the culture. Many women find comfort and joy in creating rituals together to celebrate the rhythms of nature and to mark transitions in their lives and the lives of their loved ones.

It appears to me that the intense focus on feminine spirituality at this time is a direct result of so many women having taken the hero's journey, only to find it personally empty and dangerous for humanity. Women emulated the male heroic journey because there were no other images to emulate; a woman was either "successful" in the male-oriented culture or dominated and dependent as a female. To change the economic, social, and political structures of society, we must now find new myths and heroines. This may be why so many women and men are looking to images of the Goddess and to ancient matristic cultures to understand modes of leadership that involve partnership rather than dominance and cooperation rather than greed.

"Part of the calling of women as we move out of the last years of the 20th century and into the 21st is to revive a spirituality of creativity that is not afraid of the strange beauty of the underwater world of the subconscious, and to help men out of the restricted and narrow world of provable and limited fact in which society has imprisoned them," says Madeleine L'Engle in an article in the summer 1987 issue of *Ms.*[7] She goes on to say, "My role as a feminist is not to compete with men in their world—that's too easy, and ultimately unproductive. My job is to live fully as a woman, enjoying the whole of myself and my place in the universe."

What is woman's place at this stage of our cultural development? I feel strongly that it is to heal the split that tells us that our knowings, wishes, and desires are not as important nor as valid as those of the dominant male culture. Our task is to heal the internal split that tells us to override the feelings, intuition, and dream images that inform us of the truth of life. We must have the courage to live with paradox, the strength to hold the tension of not knowing the answers, and the willingness to listen to our inner wisdom and the wisdom of the planet, which begs for change.

The heroine must become a spiritual warrior. This demands that she learn the delicate art of balance and have the patience for the slow, subtle integration of the feminine and masculine aspects of herself. She first hungers to lose her feminine self and to merge with the masculine, and once she has done this, she begins to realize that this is neither the answer nor the end. She must not discard nor give up what she has learned throughout her heroic quest, but learn to view her hard-earned skills and successes not so much as the *goal* but as one part of the entire journey. She will then begin to use these skills to work toward the larger quest of bringing people together, rather than for her own individual gain. This is the sacred marriage of the feminine and masculine—when a woman can truly serve not only the needs of others but can value and be responsive to her own needs as well. This focus on integration

and the resulting awareness of interdependence is necessary
for each one of us at this time, as we work together to preserve
the balance of life on earth.

LOT'S WIFE

But if you travel far enough, one day you will recognize
yourself coming down the road to meet yourself. And you
will say—YES.

Marion Woodman

Somewhere up the road
in another voice
and another language
she waits for another time
and the washing of the feet
while I, salt tear woman-size,
stand solidified, Lot's wife,
looking back at my flaming city
valleys and mountains and plains
away. Stand turning,
millenial weight of years turning
to the distant waiting woman
noting uncountable epochs
lives with no names
falling and tumbling
down rock encrusted hills
woman without end
her rhymings going with her
her rememberings,
her hard words, her soft words, cries,
my words, my cries, all our unheard
the ways I am hearing
the silenced sounds of women
beginning to break open
and be heard deep and wide.
Full turning, one step forward,
one more and yet another,
I move up the road
to her who I am
and am not yet.

Rhett Kelly[8]

1

Separation from the Feminine

> The mother stands for the victim in ourselves, the unfree
> woman, the martyr. Our personalities seem dangerously
> to blur and overlap with our mothers; and, in a desperate
> attempt to know where mother ends and daughter begins,
> we perform radical surgery.
>
> —Adrienne Rich, *Of Woman Born*

Both historians of motherhood and psychodynamic theorists
remind us that mothers have been held responsible, glorified,
and blamed since the Industrial Revolution for who and what
type of person their child turns out to be.[1] Mother is seen as
the prime cause of positive or negative development in a child,
without taking into account the authority and respect her role
may be accorded within her particular family system or culture. Society places enormous responsibility at the feet of
mom without giving her the financial support, prestige, and
acclaim due to a job of such momentous import for the entire
culture. There is no Academy Award for parenting. We are
slow to give credit to mother but quick to blame her for all of
society's ills. In a recent court decision in Los Angeles the
mother of a convicted gang member who lived in a crack-
infested neighborhood was criminally charged for what the
court described as her lack of adequate mothering. No mention was made of a lack of adequate fathering, education,
housing, or opportunity to grow up in a safe and secure
society.

Our society is androcentric: it sees the world from a male
perspective. Men are rewarded for their intelligence, drive,

and dependability through position, prestige, and financial gain in the world. To the degree that women are like men they are similarly but not equally rewarded. If women see themselves through a male lens and continuously measure themselves by standards of a male-defined culture, they will find themselves deficient or lacking in the qualities that men value. Women will never be men, and many women who are trying to be "as good as men" are injuring their feminine nature. Women start to define themselves in terms of deficits, in terms of what they don't have or haven't accomplished, and begin to obscure and devalue themselves as women.[2] Devaluation of women begins with mother.

According to Campbell, the task of the true hero is to shatter the established order and create the new community. In so doing the hero/heroine slays the monster of the status quo, the dragon of the old order—Holdfast, the keeper of the past.[3] On a cultural level, the established order is one of deeply entrenched patriarchal values, those of dominance and control by the stronger, more vocal, and more powerful male population. Both women and men are currently challenging patriarchal language and thought, as well as patriarchal economic, political, social, religious, and educational structures, and creating new forms. But on the personal level, the old order is embodied by the mother, and the heroine's first task toward individuation is to separate from her.

A daughter may struggle with this separation process her whole life, some making a more dramatic break than others. To distance herself from her mother and the *motherhold* on her, a woman may go through a period of rejection of all feminine qualities distorted by the cultural lens as inferior, passive, dependent, seductive, manipulative, and powerless.[4]

The degree to which a woman's mother represents the status quo, the restrictive context of sexual roles, and the deep-seated sense of female inferiority within a patriarchal society determines the degree to which a woman will seek to separate herself from her mother. As she progresses through the stages of her development and begins to understand the roots of the devaluation of the feminine in this culture, she will realize that her mother is not the cause of her feelings of inadequacy. She is merely a convenient target to blame for the confusion and low self-esteem experienced by many daughters in a culture that glorifies the masculine.

The truth is that our mothers, and their mothers before them, have been imprisoned like Lot's wife in an image projected onto them by males. Women who were mothers in the 1940s and 1950s did not have many opportunities to pursue their own goals. They were manipulated, contained, and suppressed with the assistance of advertising, girdles, and valium. It has become the task of their daughters to unbind and heal their feminine wounds.

Rejection of the Feminine

Twenty-five years ago Mary Lynne entered a women's college, determined to study higher math. She had been inspired by Sputnik in the 1950s and the subsequent challenge to American schoolchildren to study math and science. The real reason she chose math, however, was because it was a field that not many women entered at that time. "The girls I knew didn't go into math, and I wanted to be different. Most girls studied English, and I couldn't stand analyzing plots and characters. I was also tired of hearing my parents tell me to go into nursing or teaching so that I would have something to 'fall back on' if my future husband became disabled. I wasn't thinking of a future husband, and I certainly didn't want to fall back on anything! I wanted to do something important in computer sciences. I was filled with adolescent idealism. I also wanted to show my dad that I was as good as the son he had always wanted and never had."

It never occurred to her that she might not have the aptitude to succeed in higher math, in spite of low SAT scores and the advice of her college counselor to major in English. She couldn't believe it when the chair of the math department told her to choose another major at the end of her sophomore year, explaining that her low B level performance was inadequate for higher level math. "I was devastated," she recalls. "I

remember walking away dazed from our two-minute conference thinking, 'that's it, now I'm going to end up like a girl.'
Simplistically I thought that math would save me from being a
woman."

Further questioning revealed that Mary Lynne had rejected
anything associated with being feminine because she didn't
want to be like her mother, a traditional housewife whom she
saw as frustrated, controlling, angry, and rigid. "I never got
along with my mother. I think she was jealous because I did
well in school and had opportunities for higher education that
she never had. I didn't want to end up anything like her; I
wanted to be like my dad, whom I saw as flexible, successful,
and satisfied with his work. Mom was never happy. It never
occurred to me at the time that his success was at her expense
or that her own self-hate and the mixed messages she gave her
daughters had their genesis in the way that society treated
women."

Mary Lynne is now beginning to understand how her total
identification with masculine values affected her concept of
herself as a woman and how she devalued other women. "I had
a superior attitude toward other women; I wanted to think like
a man. But of course I hated myself as a woman. I closed off
large areas of myself in my quest to identify with men. I set
up a standard that demanded that for anything to be worthwhile it had to be difficult, concrete, and quantifiable. I realize
now that in rejecting the feminine in my late teens I inhibited
my growth as a woman, denied my inherent skills, and ignored
what gave me pleasure."

As she approached her forty-second birthday she had the
following dream: "I am on the back seat of a bus in Scotland.
I have fallen asleep and I awake as the bus makes its return
loop. We are on Diehard Street. It's quarter to nine in the
evening but it's still light out. The sky is illuminated by the
northern lights."

Reflecting on the dream she said, "I realize that the Diehard
Bus Line refers to my stance in life. For many years I have been
a diehard; I have steadfastly resisted anything that is considered feminine. When I couldn't succeed in math I went into

fundraising. I learned how to compete, jockey for power, and play by men's rules. But I didn't learn how to relax, how to nurture myself, or how to enjoy life. My friends tell me I'm a workaholic; I tell them I can't help it, it's how this system works. Well, I feel like I've paid my dues. I don't want to ride the Diehard Line anymore. I've sacrificed my relationship with my mother and my sisters and myself to be heroic in a man's world. It's time to get back to what's really important."

The Journey Begins: Separation from the Mother

The journey begins with the heroine's struggle to separate both physically and psychologically from her own mother and from the mother archetype, which has an even greater hold. The mother archetype is often referred to as the unconscious, particularly in its maternal aspect, involving the body and soul. The mother image represents not only one aspect of the unconscious, but it is also a symbol for the whole collective unconscious, which contains the unity of all opposites. [5]

The separation from the personal mother is a particularly intense process for a daughter because she has to separate from the one who is the same as herself. She experiences a fear of loss characterized by anxiety about being alone, separate, and different from the same-sex parent who in most cases has been her primary relationship. Separating from the mother is more complex for a daughter than a son because she "must differentiate herself from a maternal figure with whom she is to identify whereas the male child must differentiate himself from a maternal figure whose qualities and behaviors he is taught to repudiate within himself in his efforts to become masculine." [6]

Many daughters experience a conflict between wanting a freer life than their mother and wanting their mother's love and approval. They want to move beyond their mother yet fear risking the loss of their mother's love. Geographical separation may be the only way at first to resolve the tension between a daughter's need to grow up and her desire to please her mother. Girls have internalized the myth of female inferi-

Gorgon

ority in this culture and there-fore have a greater need than males for approval and vali-dation. They have difficulty risking parental displeasure: Girls' "independence—be-cause it is unexpected—is more likely to be interpreted as a rejection of the parents than is a boy's more expected rebellion."[7] This first separa-tion "often feels more like a dismemberment than a liber-ation."[8]

To accomplish this split from the mother, many young women make their mothers into the image of the archetypal vengeful, possessive, and devouring female whom they must reject to survive. A woman's actual mother may or may not embody these qualities, but the daughter internalizes them as a construct of her inner mother. According to Jung this inner mother begins to function in us as a shadow figure, an involuntary pattern that is unacceptable to our egos. We can't accept it in ourselves so we project it onto others.[9]

The image of the ogre who neglects the daughter or holds her captive is projected onto the mother who in turn must be slain. The stepmother, as in Hansel and Gretel, becomes the Wicked Witch who meets her demise in the oven. The mother/daughter relationship and the separation from the mother is so complex that in most women's literature and fairy tales the mother remains absent, dead, or villainous.[10]

The Terrible Mother and the Negative Feminine

There are two poles of expression of the archetype of Mother: the Great Mother who embodies limitless nurturance, suste-nance, and protection and the Terrible Mother who represents stasis, suffocation, and death. These archetypal models are elements of the human psyche that form in response to typical human dependency in infancy and childhood.[11] In most cases the mother is the primary object of an infant's dependency, and the task of the child is to move from this fused symbiotic relationship toward separateness, individuation, and autonomy. If the mother is perceived by the child as the source of nurture and support, the child will experience her as a positive force; if she is perceived as neglectful or smothering, the child will experience her as destructive.

In adulthood many people respond to female power and often to their own mothers in terms of the Terrible Mother aspect of the archetype. [12] They fail to see their mother's life in the context of the historical period in which she lived, her family background, and the opportunities available to women at that time. Her failings become internalized as part of the inner negative mother.

At one time a woman who was assertive, demanding, and purposeful was portrayed as a devouring bitch (e.g., Bette Davis), and a woman who complained about her lack of opportunity was seen as a passive whiner. Some daughters who were taught a subtle form of compromise and self-hate by their mothers now struggle to free themselves from this very damaging image. A young girl looks to her mother for clues as to what it means to be a woman, and if her mother is powerless the daughter feels humiliated about being female. In her desire not to be anything like her mother, she may strive for power at the expense of other needs. "Many daughters live in rage at their mother for having accepted, too readily and passively, 'whatever comes.' "[13] Until she makes this unconscious reaction conscious, the daughter will continue to function *in reaction* to her mother.

The daughter flees the devouring mother who through her jealousy and envy of her daughter's talents and potential freedom tries to imprison her. She distances herself from the mother who is overly judgmental, rigid, and unsupportive. She shuns the martyr archetype of the mother who has sacrificed her own life to be of service to her spouse and children. The mother's bitterness about her own shattered dreams may erupt into rages or passive-aggressive behavior toward the daughter who has had more opportunities. A mother who fits the stereotype of the angry, hysterical woman throwing plates at the wall as she sees her life slip away embodies the goddess Kali, who is filled with destructive rage.

Kali Ma, the Hindu Triple Goddess of creation, preserva-tion, and destruction, is known as the Dark Mother. She is the basic archetypal image of the birth-and-death Mother, simul-taneously womb and tomb, both giving life to her children and taking it away. She is the ancient symbol of the feminine portrayed in a thousand different forms. [14] According to Marija Gimbutas and Merlin Stone, matristic religions have been suppressed and devalued by patriarchal religions over the last six and a half thousand years. [15] Kali's power has been forced underground just as many women's talents, skills, and energy have been suppressed as women acquiesce to gender roles that leave them depressed and suicidal. Kali's rage, when left unexpressed or unchannelled into creative forms, becomes the dark, devouring stagnation of life unlived.

Most women can't wait to distance themselves from the angry, negative mother. We have all heard women say, "I don't want to be anything *like* my mother; I don't even want to *look* like her." Some women not only fear being like their mother; they actually fear *becoming their mother*. [16] This fear, *matrophobia*, is so deep in our culture that a mother is often left feeling totally rejected, unappreciated, and abandoned when her children leave home.

Abandoning the Mother

Abandoning the mother may feel like a betrayal not only of the woman who is the mother but of the daughter as well. "The first knowledge any woman has of warmth, nourishment, tenderness, security, sensuality, mutuality, comes from her mother. That earliest enwrapment of one female body with another can sooner or later be denied or rejected, felt as choking possessiveness, as rejection, trap, or taboo; but it is, at the beginning the whole world." [17]

Many women feel a strong desire to break away from their mother but at the same time feel intense guilt at surpassing her. Susan, a young woman in her mid-twenties, has embarked upon a career as a successful business woman and has a supportive, loving relationship with a man whom she will soon marry. Her mother has been divorced for seventeen years and has never felt the satisfaction of a career she chose for herself. She worked hard to support her children as a single mother but pursued jobs that gave her adequate financial rewards rather than a career that gave her personal fulfillment.

Now in her mid-fifties, Susan's mother lacks direction and is depressed. Her depression affects Susan's choices about expanding her business or having a child. She feels that she can never be content or successful until her mother is happy and secure, and she resents her mother's refusal to make a better life for herself.

"I've always felt that I can't be happy until Mom gets her life together," she says. "She's living with my sister, is unable to support herself financially and emotionally, and I don't think she'll ever be happy. I feel guilty that I have a relationship that works, and I know I hold myself back in business so that I'm not too successful. On the one hand I want to show her that I can do what she couldn't do, and on the other hand I'm sure my success would kill her."

Each time Susan calls her mother and tells her about a new client, her mother changes the subject and talks about her sister or her sister's children. Susan feels discounted and undermined by her mother. She mourns the fact that she will never be able to share her accomplishments or happiness with her. At the same time she feels that she has betrayed her mother because she has moved beyond her. She feels guilty about her own success and angry about her mother's failure. She experiences anxiety about being different from her mother. In the past this guilt and rage led to depression, but now she is motivated to see her mother as separate from herself and to accept her mother's choices within the context of her life circumstances.

Many daughters distance themselves from their mothers because of the mother's inability to support their daughter's individuation and success. Harriet Goldhor Lerner describes a client, Ms. J, whose mother got a migraine headache which prevented her from attending her daughter's graduation with honors from college. When Ms. J told her mother that she was thinking about getting a master's degree her mother switched topics and told her about a friend's daughter who had just gotten into medical school.[18] The mother didn't want to recognize her daughter's competence or hear about her goals for the future, because these only showed up her own inadequacy.

Unfortunately, this is a universal theme. "A mother who has been blocked from her own self-development and growth may ignore or devalue her daughter's competence, or she may do the opposite and encourage her daughter to be a 'special' or 'gifted' child whose successes the mother will vicariously enjoy."[19] Many mothers send contradictory and ambivalent messages to their daughters, such as "don't be like me but be like me" or "be successful but don't be too successful." It is no wonder that a woman rejects the feminine in favor of the masculine, which seems to value her independence and success.

Separating from the Good Mother

Perhaps the most difficult mother to leave is the mother who is a fun, nurturing, supportive, positive role model. Separating from this type of mother is akin to leaving the Garden of Eden, to leaving a state of innocence, bonding, and comfort and stepping into an uncertain world. But even the good mother who is a positive role model can unknowingly entrap her daughter. If the daughter sees her as a larger-than-life deity against whom she must measure herself, she may have to repudiate her to find her own identity.[20]

Alison is a woman in her late twenties from an established New England family. Her mother is a successful bank executive, active community member, and loving parent. She encouraged Alison throughout her Ivy League career and supported her move to the West Coast to study acting. Alison misses her terribly but doesn't want to live in the same city, in her mother's shadow. She no longer wants to hear the comparisons between her and her mother or to feel guilty about being different than her mother. After every phone conversation Alison feels a deep sense of loss of the intimacy they once shared and is depressed that she has chosen a career that is antithetical to the stable life of her mother. She and her mother are no longer the same. In her struggle to separate, Alison has begun to find the depth and texture of emotions necessary for acting. This separation with its attendant pain has been an essential first step in discovering her own artistic talents.

Many women are afraid of the term *feminine;* it has become a tainted word. Some feel that inherent in the definition is the obligation to take care of others. Society has encouraged women to live through others rather than find their own fulfillment. Catherine, a woman in her late forties, says, "The images of the feminine that were presented to us in my childhood were either of the sex object Marilyn Monroe or of the great selfless provider. Either way you ended up as the Big Tit. I'm afraid that if I'm seen as feminine, I'll lose my independence and be taken advantage of."

There is a danger in the repudiation of the feminine when the daughter who rejects the aspects of the negative feminine embodied by her mother also denies positive aspects of her own feminine nature, which are playful, sensuous, passionate, nurturing, intuitive, and creative. Many women who have had angry or emotional mothers seek to control their own anger and feelings lest they be seen as destructive and castrating. This repression of anger often prevents them from seeing the inequities in a male-defined system. Women who have seen their mothers as superstitious, religious, or old-fashioned discard the murky, mysterious, magical aspects of the feminine for cool logic and analysis. A chasm is created between the heroine and the maternal qualities within her; this chasm will have to be healed later in the journey for her to achieve wholeness.

Rejection of the Female Body
Mother
I write home

I am alone and
give me my body back.
Susan Griffin, "Mother and Child"

The rejection of the feminine occurs in both directions, from daughter to mother and from mother to daughter. As a girl enters puberty and discovers her sexuality, her mother may reject or demean her daughter's physical body. Or she may envy her daughter's youth and attractiveness, activating feelings of shame or competition in the young woman. Many girls perceive their mother's fear of them as a sign of rivalry for father's attention.

A girl's father may also be uncomfortable with his daughter's budding sexuality and spend less and less time with her. She experiences the traditional madonna/whore dichotomy; she is seen as taboo by her father and as a rival by her mother. Rather than displease her parents the young woman may shut down her emerging sexuality until she is out of the home. Or she may become so afraid of her sexuality that she marries the first man with whom she falls in love. Both her mother and her father have a hold on her body.

I suspect that this is the beginning of a woman's rejection of her instinctual body wisdom. Most women's bodies let them know when something that is going on in their lives just "doesn't feel right." But when they begin to ignore their bodies they begin to discredit their intuition in favor of their minds.

When an adolescent girl notices that her parents are uncomfortable with the outer signs of her emerging sexuality she may reject her own changing body. She may use food to numb feelings of inadequacy, or alcohol, sex, or drugs to alleviate the confusion and pain of being unacceptable. She loses the ability to recognize her body's limitations, incurring pain and illness as the split grows between body and mind. Women access their spirituality through movement and body awareness, so a denial of the body inhibits the heroine's spiritual development. She ignores her intuition and dreams and pursues the safer activities of the mind.

Sara, who is in her late thirties, is a Ph.D. candidate in

anthropology. When she entered therapy, she complained about a recurring disabling pain in her side. Her physician said there was nothing physically wrong with her, but she could not move for days in succession. We worked together with relaxation exercises to release the stress associated with writing her dissertation, and then I suggested a guided imagery exercise to ask her inner child what was happening within her body.

Sara has a strong experience of her "little girl" at age nine. This part of her wants to go outside to play upside-down on a jungle-gym. Sara spends twenty minutes playing joyfully with her younger self and then comes back inside the office and bursts into tears.

She realizes that in her academic striving she has lost this playful aspect of herself. She talks of being able to do it by herself. She says she had a wonderful relationship with a man, but he has now moved thousands of miles away to Alaska and she, the strong one, is "making it" on her own. She didn't want to be like her mom, dependent on any man. But her left side still hurts. I ask her what her body is telling her.

She says, "I have denied a very large part of myself—not only the child within, the one who once liked to play, but that part of my adult self who is nurtured outdoors in nature. I love to hike but I just haven't made time. I also love children but I have none in my life. My studies just haven't allowed for the things I like to do. I have become a strong woman, but I have no one to nurture and no knowledge or recollection of how to nurture myself. I am afraid that if I ask my family or friends for support they'll think I'm weak." Because women have been viewed as manipulative or wimpy if they acknowledge the limitations of their physical body, they have learned to override pain to keep up with the men. The female body has been both an object of desire and of scorn.

Rejection of the female body, which in our culture has its origins in the Old Testament portrayal of Eve as seductress, has been reinforced in male-dominated religions by taboos about female sexuality for over five thousand years. A woman's gender has been used as an excuse to exclude her from power by political as well as religious institutions.

Performance artist Cheri Gaulke grew up in a religious background dominated by males and male deities. At the age of four she realized that her body defined her destiny. "My father, my grandfather, my great grandfather, and my brother are all Lutheran ministers. My brother is the fourth generation. At age four I had my first feminist thought when I realized that I couldn't follow in my father's footsteps because I was a female child. At that moment I knew that Christianity had betrayed me because of my flesh. In Christianity the spirit and the flesh have been separated. Women are the flesh and the male god is the spirit. The only way to obtain spirit is to deny the flesh, transcend the flesh, and die. Well, I don't believe that."[21]

This woman's mother was an invisible force in her life. "All of my work has been about the father, trying to reclaim my power that has been robbed by males. I find inspiration in the feminine spirituality movement because the Goddess is a deity with whom I can identify. Her body and mine are one; her power and mine are one. And the men can't take that away."[22]

Rejected by Mother

A woman who has felt rejected by her mother because of adoption, illness, depression, or escape into alcohol will feel deeply unmothered and will continue to look for what she never had. She may function forever as a "daughter" looking for approval, love, attention, and acceptance from a mother who is incapable of giving these. If she experienced her mother as either absent or too busy to mother her, she may set out in search of a positive female role model, perhaps an older woman with whom she can bond.

Lila, a black woman in her late thirties, remembers her mother as a woman who was too busy having children to notice her. "She was exhausted all of the time; to her I was just a blur. But my Aunt Essie saw me. She knew who I was. She told me I was someone. She gave me hope; she taught me to believe in myself. Every time she looked me in the eye I felt beautiful. She used to say, 'Girl, you're goin' to go places. You're special.' I couldn't wait to leave home to prove that she was right."

If a woman feels alienated or rejected by her mother she may first reject the feminine and search for recognition by the father and the patriarchal culture. Men are in a position of strength, so women look to men for support to strengthen themselves. Our heroine sets out to identify with the powerful all-knowing masculine. She first learns the dizzying games of the fathers, the strategies of competition, winning, and achievement. She tries to prove that she can live up to a standard designed by white men in their image. No matter how successful she is, however, she finds that she is still undervalued and overworked.[23] She begins to question what happened to feminine values.

According to Jungian therapist Janet Dallett, "This culture's collective consciousness, composed of the myriad assumptions that dominate our values, perceptions and choices, is fundamentally masculine. The collective *un*conscious of a patriarchal society, the source of its big dreams, carries the values excluded from consciousness and therefore has a feminine (matriarchal) bias. Creative individuals today are compelled to abandon patriarchal greed and descend to the murky realm of the mothers to bring forth what presses to be born into consciousness of a new age."[24]

At this point in a woman's journey she may seek to heal the original split with her mother and to recover the mother/daughter relationship in its larger context. She will look for goddesses, heroines, and contemporary creative women with whom she can identify and who will teach her about female power and beauty and enrich her experience of her own developing authority.[25] She will ultimately find her healing in the Great Mother.

Whether we think of the Goddess as a personified Being or as energy that occurs within and between women, the image of the Goddess is an acknowledgement of female power, not dependent on men nor derived from the patriarchal vision of women. . . . The Goddess reflects

back to us what has been so missing in our culture:
positive images of our power, our bodies, our wills, our
mothers. To look at the Goddess is to remember ourselves, to imagine ourselves whole. [26]

2

Identification with the Masculine

Daughters of the Father

In spite of the successes achieved by the women's movement, the prevailing myth in our culture is that certain people, positions, and events have more inherent value than others. These people, positions, and events are usually masculine or male-defined. Male norms have become the social standard for leadership, personal autonomy, and success in this culture, and in comparison women find themselves perceived as lacking in competence, intelligence, and power.

The girl observes this as she grows up and wants to identify with the glamour, prestige, authority, independence, and money controlled by men. Many high-achieving women are considered *daughters of the father* because they seek the approval and power of that first male model. Somehow mother's approval doesn't matter as much, father defines the feminine, and this affects her sexuality, her ability to relate to men, and her ability to pursue success in the world. Whether a woman feels that it is alright to be ambitious, to have power, to make money, or to have a successful relationship with a man derives from her relationship with her father.

Lynda Schmidt defines a father's daughter as "the daughter with a powerful, positive relationship with her father, probably to the exclusion of her mother. Such a young woman will orient herself around men as she grows up, and will have a somewhat deprecatory attitude toward women. Father's daughters organize their lives around the masculine principle, either remaining connected to an outer man or being driven from within by a masculine mode. They may find a male mentor or guide, but they may have, at the same time, trouble taking orders from a man or accepting teaching from one."[1]

Psychologists who study motivation have found that many successful women had fathers who nurtured their talent and made them feel attractive and loved at an early age. Marjorie Lozoff, a San Francisco Bay Area social scientist who conducted a four-year study on women's career success, concluded that women were more likely to be self-determining "when the fathers treated the daughters as if they were interesting people, worthy and deserving of respect and encouragement."[2] Women thus treated "did not feel their femininity was endangered by the development of talent."[3] Such fathers took an active interest in their daughter's lives and also encouraged their daughters to take an active interest in their own professional lives or avocations in politics, sports, or the arts.

Former congresswoman Yvonne Brathwaite Burke, whose father devoted his life to the Service Employees International Union, walked in her first picket line when she was fourteen. Her father was a janitor at MGM for twenty-eight years, and his home was always full of union activists. His union provided Burke with a scholarship to UCLA and the USC law school.

Watching her father's organizing efforts, she became aware "of what it means to really fight for something. He believed in the continuing struggle and was very dedicated, although he was out of work for months. He felt it was the necessary thing to do."[4] His dedication had enormous impact on her.

"I was very interested in the idea of struggle and what my father was going through. I knew it was very difficult for him, and certainly a sacrifice, but he believed in it. He discussed his union work with me, and I was aware of all the details. Later, he was very supportive of my becoming a lawyer and going into politics. He influenced me to get involved."[5] Burke's mother, a real estate agent, was not as enthusiastic about her daughter getting into politics because she did not want her embroiled in controversy. She encouraged her daughter to be a teacher, but Burke wanted to be more active and involved in solving conflict.

Former San Francisco mayor Dianne Feinstein also learned from her father's example about the intricacies of bureaucracies and how to be diplomatic, stick up for her rights, and be strong and persistent. Her father worked enthusiastically on her campaigns and did everything from fundraising to bringing doughnuts to her office staff. As a doctor he had a strong commitment to public service, and, in spite of suffering from cancer, he worked up until the time of his death. He taught his daughter about staying-power and motivation. Feinstein was strengthened by her father's enduring faith in her capabilities. "He always had high expectations for me. Deep within him he believed that whatever I reached for was attainable, while I did not always believe it."[6]

A young girl's relationship with her father helps her to see the world through his eyes and to see herself reflected by him. As she seeks his approval and acceptance, she measures her own competence, intelligence, and self-worth in relation to him and to other men. Approval and encouragement by a girl's father lead to positive ego development. Both Feinstein and Burke remember close, easy relationships with their fathers. "Neither woman felt she was sacrificing her femininity by competing in a male-dominated field."[7]

Women who have felt accepted by their fathers have confidence that they will be accepted by the world. They also develop a positive relationship to their masculine nature. They have an inner masculine figure who likes them just as they are. This positive inner male or animus figure will support their creative efforts in an accepting, nonjudgmental way.

Linda Leonard describes her fantasy of the positive inner masculine figure. She calls him the Man with Heart. He is "caring, warm, and strong," unafraid of anger, intimacy, and love. "He stays by me and is patient. But he initiates, confronts, and moves on as well. He is stable and enduring. Yet his stability comes from flowing with the stream of life, from being in the moment. He plays and works and enjoys both modes of being. He feels at home wherever he is—in the inner spaces or the outer world. He is a man of the earth—instinctual and sexy. He is a man of the spirit—soaring and

creative."[8] This inner figure is engendered by a positive relationship with a woman's father or father figure. The inner male
will be a supportive guide throughout the heroine's journey.

Father as Ally

Dr. Alexandra Symonds of the New York University School of
Medicine made a study of women who had high commitments
to their work and found that they had fathers who stressed the
importance of education and taught them how to play the
games of the business world. They coached their daughters to
keep going in spite of failure and normal feelings of anxiety.
They inspired them to be responsible for their own lives.
These women were encouraged at an early age to achieve
rather than to be dependent.

Symonds found that it is fathers who can best cultivate
healthy competence in their daughters. Although I don't agree
with her findings and feel that mothers have as much to do
with the building of their daughters' competence, I do agree
with her statement that "if fathers give their daughters the kind
of encouragement they give their sons, in sports, in sustained
effort, in being self-sufficient, then even if the girls don't
accomplish something outstanding, they will have developed
qualities which will be important the rest of their lives. Their
fathers can help them very much instead of patting them on
the head and saying, 'Aren't you cute.' That is not enough."[9]

Women who have received such support have confidence to
move *toward* something. They choose a career track that has
definable goals and specific steps to follow—law, medicine,
business, education, or arts administration, to name just a few.
Women whose fathers did not support their ideas and dreams
for the future or who gave them the impression that they
lacked the ability to carry them out meander through life and
may *back into* success.

Some women who are successful try not only to emulate
their fathers but consciously set out *not* to be like their
mothers, whom they perceive as dependent, helpless, or
hypercritical. In cases where a mother is chronically de-

The Birth of Athena

pressed, ill, or alcoholic the daughter allies herself with her father, ignoring her mother who becomes the shadow in the upstairs bedroom. The father then carries the power not only in the outside world but in her inner world as well.

Daddy's Girl: Absorption of the Feminine

The elimination of the mother and identification with the father is well illustrated in the story of Athena, daughter of Metis and Zeus. Zeus's absorption of Metis can also be seen to represent the period of transition in Greek cultural history from a matrilineal society to a masculine, ego-dominated world.

Athena sprang out of Zeus's head as a full-grown woman, wearing flashing gold armor, holding a sharp spear in one

hand, and emitting a mighty war cry. Following this dramatic
birth Athena associated herself with Zeus, acknowledging him
as her sole parent. The goddess never acknowledged her
mother, Metis. In fact, Athena seemed ignorant of the fact
that she had a mother.

> As Hesiod recounts, Metis was Zeus's first royal consort,
> an ocean deity who was known for her wisdom. When
> Metis was pregnant with Athena, Zeus tricked her into
> becoming small and swallowed her. It was predicted that
> Metis would have two very special children: a daughter
> equal to Zeus in courage and wise counsel, and a son, a
> boy of all-conquering heart, who would become king of
> gods and men. By swallowing Metis, Zeus thwarted fate
> and took over her attributes as his own. [10]

Athena was the beautiful warrior goddess who protected her
Greek heroes in battle. She was the goddess of wisdom and
crafts, a master strategist, diplomat, and weaver, and patroness
of cities and civilization. She helped Jason and the Argonauts
build their ship before setting out to capture the Golden
Fleece and assisted the Greeks in bringing down Troy. She
sided with the patriarchy in casting the deciding vote to free
Orestes, who had killed his mother, Clytemnestra, to avenge
the murder of his father, Agamemnon, after the Trojan War.
In doing so she ranked patriarchal values over maternal bonds.

An "Athena woman" is a father's daughter; she depreciates
her own mother and identifies with her father. She is bright
and ambitious and gets things done. She has little value for
emotional relationship; she lacks empathy and compassion for
vulnerability. If she does not take the time to discover her
mother's strengths and reclaim her deep connection to the
maternal bond, she may never heal her separation from the
feminine. Metis was not the last mother to be swallowed by
male ego, and Athena was not the last daughter who discarded
her mother in favor of Dad. I write this book in part to
understand and heal the split that occurred between my
mother and myself.

As a young girl I saw my father as a god. I couldn't wait for him to come home from work; he was funny, intelligent, creative, and, as an advertising executive, he had power in the world. He was one of the daddies who came home from World War II ambitious to partake of the economic opportunities open to bright young men. He worked long hours in a big building in Manhattan, won national awards, and was a mentor to the male talent in his agency.

To me he could do no wrong; he was the love of my life. I missed him in the evening because he rarely came home for dinner, but sometimes I saw him in the early morning before I left for school. His mysterious comings and goings early in the morning and late at night gave him mythic proportions in my young eyes. He must be doing "important work," I thought—probably the work of gods!

When he was home I wanted his attention, his approval, his conversation. I acted smart and I listened. I loved going to the hardware store with him and to the lumber yard. He was a person who could never sit still; at home he always worked on one project or another. To this day I still associate the smell of freshly cut wood with my father.

When I turned thirteen I began to work summers in his office. He was always very proud of me because I was a top student, and he showed me off around the office. He told me about his business and the value of making it on his own. He talked about the value of education because as a self-taught man he regretted the lack of formal education in his own life.

He discouraged my interest in pursuing the advertising field, however; he said it was "no place for girls." It was his opinion that women had too many mood swings for media work. The only career I can remember him thinking was appropriate for girls was copywriting, because he felt that women could do that at home while they took care of the family. I secretly planned to show him that I was different.

Unlike many of my teenage girlfriends' fathers, mine was willing to listen to my feelings; this was desperately important to me because I could not talk with my mother. Through him I could hear myself. I felt fortunate that I could tell him anything—or at least I *thought* I could. He didn't like to hear

my confusion about my mother's violent outbursts; he told me
to be more understanding and to be patient with her.

I dream that I go to an Al-Anon meeting and Peg, a friend
of mine who is a psychiatrist, is there. She sits directly across
from me and holds my hands as I talk to the group. She gives
me so much time to share that the other women start to
protest. She says, "There must be enormous sadness for you
that your father was not present, that he was so busy working
that he couldn't help you out."

I'm surprised at her words, surprised that she addresses my
sadness in regard to my father, because I had always identified
my mother as the problem. I saw her as the villain and wanted
my dad to rescue me, a recurring theme for the traditional
undifferentiated heroine. I idolized my father, saw him as my
savior, and performed well the role of the pretty, intelligent
daughter waiting for my prince to come. He never succeeded
in rescuing me, however. I realized many years later that he
had abandoned both me and my mother so that he could do
important things in the world.

The Father Quest: Gathering Allies

During the second stage of the heroine's journey a woman
wishes to identify with the masculine or to be rescued by the
masculine. When a woman decides to break with established
images of the feminine she inevitably begins the traditional
hero's journey. She puts on her armor, mounts her modern-
day steed, leaves loved ones behind, and goes in search of the
golden treasure. She fine-tunes the skills of logos. She looks
for clearly defined routes to success. She sees the male world
as healthy, fun-loving, and action-oriented. Men get things
done. This fuels her own ambition.

This is an important period in the development of a woman's
ego. Our heroine looks for role models who can show her the
steps along the way. These male allies may take the form of a
father, boyfriend, teacher, manager, or coach; of the institution granting the degree or salary she seeks; or of a minister,
rabbi, priest, or God. The ally may also be a male-identified

woman, perhaps an older childless woman who has played by team rules and successfully made her way to the top.

Jill Barad, the executive vice-president of marketing, world-wide product design and development at Mattel Toys, one of the highest-ranking female executives in corporate America, credits her success not only to teamwork and her ability to motivate employees, but also to the several mentors to whom she could turn over the years for advice. She describes her management style, which is uniquely her own, as one that draws on her sensitivity and strong intuitive side as well as the use of constructive feedback, which are basic values she learned from her parents. She grew up in a creative household with a lot of mental stimulation and was fortunate to have a father who always told her, "You can be anything you want to be—just be good at it. Put your mind to it, learn what you need to, and go for it!"[11]

"Most women seek power and authority either by becoming like men or by becoming liked by men."[12] This is not such a negative thing at first because seeking male validation is a healthy transition from fusion with the mother to greater independence in a patriarchal society. The young woman who identifies with what could be considered positive father qualities, such as discipline, decision-making, direction, courage, power, and self-valuation, finds herself achieving success in the world.

This can be very damaging, however, if a woman believes that she does not exist except in the mirror of male attention or male definition. In *Alice's Adventures in Wonderland* Lewis Carroll parodies the belief that those with political power can define the identities of the powerless.[13] Tweedledum and Tweedledee tell Alice that she exists solely in the Red King's imagination:

> "He's dreaming now," said Tweedledee, "and what do you think he's dreaming about?"
> Alice said, "Nobody can guess that."
> "Why about you!" Tweedledee exclaimed, clapping his hands triumphantly. "And if he left off dreaming about you, where do you suppose you'd be?"

"Where I am now, of course," said Alice.

"You'd be nowhere. Why, you're only a sort of thing in his dream!"

"If that there King was to wake," added Tweedledum, "you'd go out—bang!—just like a candle!"[14]

Lack of a Positive Masculine Ally

Approval and encouragement by the father or other father substitutes usually lead to a woman's positive ego development; but lack of genuine involvement or negative involvement on the part of the father, stepfather, uncle, or grandfather deeply wounds a woman's sense of her self. It can lead to over-compensation and perfectionism or virtually paralyze her development. When a father is absent or indifferent to his daughter he indicates his disinterest, disappointment, and disapproval, which can be as damaging to the heroine as explicit negative judgments or overprotectiveness.

In *The Female Hero in American and British Literature*, Carol Pearson and Katherine Pope quote from the diary of Canadian artist Emily Carr, whose father was physically present but emotionally indifferent to her and to her mother. In her late sixties she was still grappling with this indifferent god.

> Sixty-six years ago tonight I was hardly me. . . . I wonder what Father felt. I can't imagine him being half as interested as Mother. More to Father's taste was a nice juicy steak served piping on the great pewter hotwater dish. That made his eyes twinkle. I wonder if he ever succored Mother up with a tender word or two after she'd been through a birth or whether he was as rigid as ever, waiting for her to buck up and wait on him. He ignored new babies until they were old enough to admire him, old enough to have wills to break.[15]

Inadequate attention from a father on the personal level or from a mentor on the cultural level results in what Linda Leonard calls the "armored Amazon."

In reacting against the negligent father such women often identify on the ego level with the masculine or fathering functions themselves. Since their fathers did not give them what they needed, they find they have to do it themselves. . . . The armor protects them positively insofar as it helps them develop professionally and enables them to have a voice in the world of affairs. But insofar as the armor shields them from their own feminine feelings and their soft side, these women tend to become alienated from their own creativity, from healthy relationships with men, and from the spontaneity and vitality of living in the moment. [16]

This type of woman will be seen as professionally successful but difficult to trust in the emotional or relational arena. Her inner masculine figure is not a man with heart but a greedy tyrant that never lets up. Nothing she does is ever enough; he drives her forward "more, better, faster" with no recognition of her longings to be loved, to feel satisfied, or even to rest.

Danielle is a woman in her early thirties who runs a highly competitive commercial real estate firm. She is tall, intelligent, beautiful, and sexy and uses all of these attributes to her advantage in business. She is also as hard as nails. She is in love with the image of her father, now dead for three years, who was a successful European entrepreneur. He was a powerfully built man and a commanding presence; he controlled the family with an iron fist.

He lavished praise on Danielle for her looks and intelligence, told her to stay away from sex because it was dirty, and spoke to her about his travails and successes in the business world. She was his confidante. When Danielle was in her teens, he divorced her mother. The mother had been physically and emotionally abusive to Danielle during her childhood and had become increasingly dysfunctional and alcoholic as Danielle entered adolescence. The father remarried a young woman only slightly older than Danielle, whom he treated as little more than a sexual servant. He also had a series of affairs which everyone knew about.

Danielle wanted to join his business but he would not allow it, giving her the impression that business was not for girls. After his death she started her own business. She longed to show herself that she could do it. She mourned deeply for the things that he never taught her and took it out on all the men with whom she related either professionally or personally. When she lost a business account because of her rudeness and aggression, she blamed it on the client for not being able to accept an assertive woman.

When Danielle experienced failures in her business she raged that "this would never have happened if my father was alive; he would have helped me." She denied the fact that he had never supported her independent efforts during his lifetime. She trusted no one and started to develop a series of cervical and vaginal infections. She was cut off from her soft feminine side and had great disdain for most women, whom she categorized as ignorant, conniving, and destructive.

Her greatest fear related to her recurring genital infections, and she blamed the men with whom she was involved for their inability to have a serious, sustained relationship. Using a guided imagery exercise I encouraged her to communicate with the raw sores around her vagina. As she did so she touched the core of her anger. "I'm outraged because I had to become heroic at a very early age to combat my mother. I was too little to deal with her craziness. The message from my father was to ignore her while he went away to do powerful things in the world. He didn't protect me.

"Trying to make it in the outside world is beyond my grasp. Trying to compete is beyond my comprehension. I end up feeling superior and impatient with people because I have always held a grandiose position of power in my family, looking down at my inadequate, crazy mother and being the confidante of my father. I am crippled. I no longer have the king's ear; he's dead. And what did he give me? A false sense of importance because I was his confidante. I was no more than a glorified handservant.

"Now I don't know how to show real care for anyone, and I'm too afraid to compete in the work world. I want to start at the top. I don't know how to run this business effectively, and I certainly don't want to work my way up in someone else's firm. I have trouble negotiating with other people, especially men, whom I just don't trust."

Danielle's father not only sabotaged her goals to be a successful businesswoman but robbed her of the possibility for success in relationship as well. He displayed his disdain for women through his treatment of his wives and Danielle's half-sisters. Her older sister committed suicide as a teen. He used all of the women in his life for his own purposes, including Danielle, who thought she was exempt. She realizes now, as she continues the work to heal herself, that he still has a grip on her sexuality.

Many women who strive to succeed in business to prove their worth to their fathers have difficulty sustaining success, even if they have had educational backgrounds to support their career. If their fathers gave them direct or indirect messages that women don't belong in business they internalize the message that actual achievement is inconsistent with the feminine sex-role stereotype. [17]

Addiction to Perfection

A young woman may appear to succeed while bleeding herself dry internally. Because of an innate fear of female inferiority, many young women become addicted to perfection, overcompensating, and overworking because they are different than men.

> We live in a culture that does not trust process and is intolerant of diversity. Therefore we are all expected to be perfect, and beyond that, to be perfect in similar—if not the same—ways to one another. We are supposed to "live up" to standards of virtue, achievement, intelligence, and physical attractiveness. If we do not, then we are expected to repent, work harder, study, diet, exercise, and wear better clothes until we fit the prevailing image of an ideal person. Thus, our unique qualities [in this case being female] are likely to be defined as "the problem" that we need to solve to be OK. [18]

Some women take great pride in learning how to think like men, how to compete with them, and how to beat them at their own game. Such women become heroic, but many are left with a gnawing sensation that they will never be *enough*. They continue to do more, out of the need to be the same as men. Having grown up in a Catholic household I often wonder if a woman's sense of lack stems from the fact that she was not made in the image of God. The experience many girls have with their fathers is the same they have with the father God: loved but held apart, even feared, because they have different genitalia.

Nancy is a woman in her early forties who has returned to law school after twenty years as a performer and political activist. When she does her assignments for school she realizes that she wastes an enormous amount of time and energy trying to do each assignment perfectly. She puts much more effort into each problem than is required. Because of this she never has enough time to finish all of her work, and her grades reflect assignments finished late. Nancy doesn't lack intelligence or the ability to do the work; she overdoes it.

When I ask her who she writes the perfect answers for, she responds, "Dad." She tells me about the memory of a recurring dialogue she had with her late father when she was a little girl. He was a truck driver with a great sense of humor who treated her, the first daughter, like a son. "Well, I wish you were a boy," he'd say, "but since you're not, what's nine times nine?"

"I always had the right answer to any question he asked," recalls Nancy. "I memorized sports statistics, the longest words in the dictionary, and the capital of every state so I would never be off-guard. It was great for my memory, but I had no concept of what it meant to be a girl. All I knew was that something was wrong with me because I wasn't a boy, and I had to figure out how to make up for that."

Nancy was defined by her father's ideal of what it was to be a female. Since she already lacked the physical equipment to be male, the next best thing was to be smart and do things perfectly. My own father put it this way: "If you can't do it right, don't do it at all"—which I internalized as a dictum not to try anything unless I could ace it.

Learning the Rules of the Game with Dad

Little girls learn early on which games to play for their father's approval and attention. They may have to act smart, cute, coy, or be seductive. Power and authority arc daddy issues inside the bedroom as well as out. The first man a girl flirts with is her daddy. How he responds to her is critical to a girl's sexual development. A father's warmth, playfulness, and love are very important to a girl's healthy sexuality; otherwise, her primary love object will remain her first attachment, her mother. On the other hand, a father's dominance, possessiveness, and criticism can undermine or destroy a girl's heterosexual development.

More abusive is the father who ignores his natural role as protector of his young daughter's sexuality and, because of a need for male dominance, violates her normal sexual development through incest. She will spend the rest of her life reclaiming her sexuality and the fact that as a woman she *does have rights.*

Other girl children learn that it is best not to act too smart around Dad. They might become a target for ridicule, criticism, disapproval, or physical abuse. They learn not to be "smarty pants" around men who can't fill the pants in the family. They quickly learn to let Dad win in cards, checkers, or free throws in basketball and tennis. They forget their own ambitions and become women who make their bosses look good. They end up feeling bitter, passive, and cynical about what has happened to their lives.

Girls who suffered from the denial of positive attention from their fathers in childhood look for him in each relationship they have. Loretta, a woman in her late thirties, idolized her handsome sportscaster father but was unable to get his attention. She grew up with three athletic brothers who monopolized his interest. As a girl she was quiet and dreamy and loved to spend her time in the woods, but she had no athletic ability and little interest in sports. Loretta's father made fun of the stories she wrote and ridiculed the games she played with her animals. Her mother was quiet and depressed. Loretta didn't know how to enter the all-male world around her so she married into it.

"My first husband was a baseball player in the minors, so I went to the games and invited my dad to sit in the box with me. Dad followed my husband's career closely but had no interest in mine, and the more time I spent with Jon off-season, the more I realized that we had nothing in common. So I married Mike. He was older and looked just like my dad. He was also an athlete but not a professional one, so I thought things would be different. He was a writer like me, but he always told me I had no talent. After three years of listening to that, I realized I was beginning to disappear just like my mother.

"I left Mike, and it took me awhile to heal, but after we had been apart for a year I woke up to the fact that I was marrying these guys in an effort to fill a giant hole left by my dad's rejection of me. I stopped seeing men altogether and focused on my writing. Now I'm seeing a high-school teacher who looks nothing like my dad, doesn't follow sports, and is interested in what I have to say. We really enjoy each other; it's the first time I've felt good about being a woman. I don't know if I'll remarry, but I do know that I no longer need to look for Dad."

Putting the Patriarchy on Notice

Part of the heroine's quest is to find her work in the world, which enables her to find her identity. It is important for a woman to know that she can survive without dependence on parents or others so that she can express her heart, mind, and soul. Skills learned during this first part of the heroic quest establish a woman's competence in the world.

I do not mean to imply that the qualities needed for success and achievement are solely shaped by the masculine or that the father is the primary role model for these qualities in the world. The fact is, however, that the system within which we live and work is primarily a patriarchal system, valuing men more than women. This is certainly changing, but change is slow.

The continuing devaluation of women on the outer level affects how a woman feels about herself inwardly and how she perceives the feminine. Women are no longer willing to be perceived as inferior. At the present time women are going through a profound inner change in response to the patriarchy. This inner movement is gradually being reflected in current changes in social policy.

While I know that we have a long way to go to achieve gender and racial equality, young girls who grow up today in families where feminine values are honored will bring a focus on healthier family and societal relationships tomorrow. May their inner masculine figure be a Man with Heart.

3

The Road of Trials

Confronting Ogres and Dragons

The heroine crosses the threshold, leaves the safety of her parents' home, and goes in search of her self. She journeys up hills and down valleys, wades in rivers and streams, crosses dry deserts and dark forests, and enters the labyrinth to find what is at the center of her self. Along the way she meets ogres who trick her into going down dead ends, adversaries who challenge her cunning and resolve, and obstacles which she must avoid, circumscribe, or overcome. She needs a lamp, a lot of thread, and all of her wits about her to make this journey.

But I am getting ahead of myself. Why is she out there meandering around in the labyrinth at night anyway? What is the treasure she is looking for, and who is the dragon guarding it?

She is alone at night metaphorically, wandering the road of trials to discover her strengths and abilities and uncover and overcome her weaknesses. That is what leaving home and taking the journey is all about. *Home* is the safety and security of the known. School, a new job, travel, and relationship all provide her with opportunities to look at and experience her positive qualities as well as the negative aspects of herself that she projects onto others. No longer can she blame parents, siblings, friends, lovers, and her boss for the outcome of her life; now it is time to look at herself. Her task is to take the sword of *her* truth, find the sound of *her* voice, and choose the

Challenging Myth III. Painting by Nancy Ann Jones.

path of *her* destiny. Thus she will find the treasure of her seeking.

She will encounter obstructions along the way both in her outer rational world as well as in the inner world of the psyche. The outer road of trials will take her through the expected obstacle course that leads to academic degrees, promotions, prestigious titles, marriage, and financial success. Dragons will be there to guard the boon, telling her she can't possibly succeed, she doesn't really want to do that anyway, and there are many more qualified people ahead of her. These dragons will seem at times daunting, resembling her parents, teachers, and bosses.

The most challenging dragon of all, however, is the societal reptile that smiles and says, "Yes dear, you can do anything you want to do," while continuing to sabotage her progress with few opportunities, low salaries, inadequate child care, and slow promotions. What this dragon really means is, "Yes dear, you can do anything you want to do as long as you do what *we* want you to do."

Ogres will appear on her path to test her endurance, her decisiveness, and her ability to set limits. Coworkers will nettle her, licensing boards will change their requirements, and lovers will declare that they didn't really love her in the first place. She will be tempted by games of sex and manipulation disguised as requirements for power, achievement, and love. She will be flattered into thinking she has arrived in the land of power and independence when all she has received are the talismans of success.

Along the inner journey she will encounter the forces of her own self-doubt, self-hate, indecisiveness, paralysis, and fear. The outer world might tell her she can do it, but she battles with demons that tell her she can't. "I can't do it, I'm a fraud." . . . "If they ever knew what I was really like they'd never put their trust in me." . . . "I don't want to stand out; if I succeed they'll hate me." . . . "It was so much better when I was taken care of." . . . "I don't deserve it." . . . "If I was a real woman I'd want to get married and have kids."

The litany goes on and serves to undermine her clarity, self-confidence, ambition, and self-worth. The dragons that jealously guard the myth of dependency, the myth of female inferiority, and the myth of romantic love are fearsome opponents. This is not a journey for cowards; it takes enormous courage to plumb one's depths.

The Myth of Dependency

Dependency and *needs*: both are dirty words for women. Although dependency is a normal developmental stage for both girls and boys, the word *dependent* is most often associated with women. Girls are not encouraged toward independence; they are not supported to be autonomous the way boys are. "On the contrary, girls are encouraged to maintain their dependent relationships to parents and family, and after marriage transfer them to husband and children."[1]

Women are expected to take care of the dependency needs of others; they are trained from girlhood to anticipate these needs. They have heard their mothers say, "You must be thirsty, can I get you a cold drink?" . . . "You've had a long day, you must be tired. Do you want to lie down before dinner?" . . . "You must be so disappointed that you didn't get on the team."

As they learn to anticipate others' needs they consciously or unconsciously expect that their needs will be anticipated and taken care of as well. When a woman discovers that her needs are *not* being considered she feels that something is wrong with *her*. She may actually feel shame that she has needs too.

If a woman has to ask to have a need met, she is perceived as demanding, needy, and dependent by others as well as herself. The truth is, however, that she merely has normal needs which may not have been met by a spouse, lover, friend, or child.[2] These normal needs may include time to herself, a room of her own, someone to listen, a loving embrace, or the opportunity to pursue her talents. When normal needs are denied she begins to feel that she has no *right* to pursue activities that would fill her own needs and wants. Somehow she begins to expect that she has no rights at all.

Some women act dependent to bolster their partner's ego or to protect him. There is an unspoken rule in the relationship that for the husband to be strong the woman has to be weak. This myth says that if one partner diminishes herself the other partner can be successful; his power comes at the expense of her weakness. This myth is not limited to heterosexual relationships. Our heroine gives up *herself* so that the other— husband, coworker, lover, or child—may gain self. This unconscious "gift" or sacrifice of self to the other gives her a sense of self-worth and helps maintain equilibrium in the system. In *Women in Therapy,* Harriet Lerner writes:

> Underlying the passive-dependent stance of many women is the unconscious motivation to bolster and protect another person as well as the unconscious conviction that one must remain in a position of relative weakness for one's most important relationships to survive. Even intellectually liberated women unconsciously feel frightened and guilty about "hurting" others, especially men, when fully exercising their capacity for independent thinking and action. In reality, women who do begin to define more clearly the terms of their own lives are frequently accused of diminishing men, hurting children, or in some way being destructive to others. [3]

This attitude that the "other" comes first is often internalized as an unspoken vow by a woman, even if her partner does not expect or want it. It seeps into the unconscious of a little girl as she watches the dynamics of her family. She sees her mother defer her needs and she learns to do that too. It gets interesting when the "other" that vies for her attention is part of herself. Then she has to resolve an insistent internal conflict that defies resolution.

Such is the experience of Lynne, a writer in her early forties whose husband is a recovering cocaine addict. During a period of excessive drug use the couple separated and Lynne pursued her screenwriting career with great success. Now that they are reconciled and he is in recovery, she constantly wrestles with her own need to write, be independent, and contribute to the family income on one hand; and the voice that tells her on the other that the pursuit of her career puts her family at risk.

Lynne is held in the grip of the Two-Headed Dragon, a slimy creature which bickers and moans about who is getting the greater share of her time and energy. The Writer never gets enough and the Mother is left feeling unappreciated and unloved. Their ongoing struggle depletes Lynne's creativity and leaves her in a state of mental and emotional exhaustion.

I asked Lynne to write a dialogue between the two heads of this dragon. In the following exchange she notes that the

Mother speaks in a soft, apologetic voice and the Writer has a strong, angry voice. Sometimes they get confused about who they are.

The Two-Headed Dragon

WRITER: Get to work. You're late. And you don't have enough time as it is. Besides, it takes you so long to warm up. Snap out of it. Shake it off. Let go of that other person.

MOTHER: But I am that other person. Me. I am the real you.

WRITER: I let you think that. That's all.

MOTHER: I am the person that gets up in the morning. And makes the beds. Feeds the kids. Washes the dishes. Picks up the house. I have to do it.

WRITER: Why? It slows me down. It gets in my way.

MOTHER: If it wasn't for me—

WRITER: If it wasn't for you, I'd have more time.

MOTHER: If it wasn't for me, you'd have given up. I gave you a reason to go on, a reason to be. I am your anchor.

WRITER: You're taking me under. You drown me in your needs. You use me up. You make me tired in the morning. I can't stop thinking about you. And your needs. Their needs. You can't tell the difference. You use me up. You give me your leftovers.

MOTHER: I'm the one who's used up. There's never enough of me. I can't do enough. They scream for more. More me. They. The kids, the husband, the others. More more more. I want to make them happy. It's so hard. They always want more. You want more.

WRITER: I deserve more.

MOTHER: I deserve more. I deserve to be alive. To pee when I want to. When I have to. To pee alone. To get fresh air. To dance if I want to.

WRITER: You can't do that. It cuts into my time. I keep you alive. I am your fresh air. If it wasn't for me, you'd have caved in long ago.

MOTHER: If it wasn't for me, you'd have given up—

WRITER: Don't interrupt me—

MOTHER: You interrupted *me*—

WRITER: I'm supposed to—I deserve to—

MOTHER: And I deserve more. I want more—

WRITER: What? What do you want?

MOTHER: Time!

WRITER: I want more time! You can't have any more!

MOTHER: I want to feel good—forget good. Better! I'll settle for better!

WRITER: I want it more than you. When you feel good, I feel good. And I can get on with things—

MOTHER: Then let me feel good. About me.

WRITER: That's your problem. Good luck, sucker.

MOTHER: I need it—I need more—

WRITER: Time? Then sleep less.

MOTHER: But I'm so tired—

WRITER: Then don't mess with me. Stay out of my way. Keep quiet.

MOTHER: I can't.

WRITER: I know. Neither can I.

This exhausting dialogue is repeated over and over again with slight variations within each woman who has to fight to maintain her *self*. It is reinforced by cultural and familial injunctions that everyone else comes first. Consideration of her autonomy, growth, and development comes second or third or fourth.

To confront this myth of dependency our heroine has to uncover the tacit attitudes of her family about female dependence and how she may or may not have internalized those to keep the system in balance. There is considerable guilt and anxiety experienced by women who surpass their mothers. They experience their success as a betrayal of the mother/daughter relationship and feel guilty for having left their mother behind.

It is also important for the heroine to understand and appreciate the function served by her dependence both in past as well as present relationships. She may be unconscious of her need to protect others from her autonomy and success. As she realizes this she will need patience with herself to affirm her growth. She also has to recognize that she has healthy needs that deserve fulfillment. If she is in a relationship, school, or work situation that does not meet her needs, then she has the right to get out.

In the last twenty years there has been a great deal of research conducted on the changing family in this culture and a re-examination of the roles of women and men. The results of these studies show that "virtually all women today share a basic core of commitment to family and to their own equality within and beyond it, as long as family and equality are not seen to be in conflict."[4]

In this generation women have had to confront choices involving motherhood and career that no generation of women before them has had to examine. Women who have chosen to postpone motherhood for career have found themselves in the uncomfortable position in their mid- to late thirties of either not having found a spouse with whom to raise a family or of being reluctant to give up the prestige, power, and financial rewards they have achieved at work.

In coming to terms with these types of issues—the need for autonomy and the need for generativity—women require an attitude change on the part of society, and they need the assistance of men. Flexible roles in the family and business and legislative policies that reflect these will ultimately change the way dependency is viewed and experienced by women. Our heroine will no longer have to give herself away for the growth and development of others. Autonomy, achievement, *and* nurturance will be accepted qualities for women.

The Myth of Female Inferiority

The best slave
does not need to be beaten.
She beats herself.

Not with a leather whip,
or with sticks or twigs,
not with a blackjack
or a billy club,
but with the fine whip
of her own tongue
& the subtle beating
of her mind against her mind.

For who can hate her half so well
as she hates herself?
and who can match the finesse
of her self-abuse?

Years of training
are required for this.

. . . .
Erica Jong, "Alcestis on the
Poetry Circuit"

Because society denigrates feminine qualities a woman is not likely to value herself as a woman. She is seen and sees herself as lacking and operates out of the myth of inferiority. She looks around and sees men achieving—men who are not as intelligent, creative, or as ambitious as she. This confuses her, but it confirms what she has observed about cultural attitudes: "Male is better." . . . "Women have no intrinsic value of their own—their value comes in relationship to men and to children." She buys into that myth and evaluates her skills and knowledge through the lens of deficit thinking: "If I just do more . . . if I try harder . . . if I'm a good girl . . . if I get that degree . . . if I wear that suit . . . if I drive that car. If . . . if . . . if . . . then I will be okay."

She internalizes a feeling of self-loathing, and the voice of her self-hate begins to sound very much like her mother and father. This inner critic may be personified as either a male Ogre Tyrant or as a female Wicked Witch, either of whom will have to be slain. Because women have been socialized to express rage against themselves, the first target of their disdain will be mother.[5] As mentioned before, we see this reflected in the treatment of mothers in most fairy tales; they all seem to meet an untimely or gruesome death. I usually suggest to my women clients that instead they send their nagging female critics on extended holiday to Hawaii for rest and relaxation.

Slaying the Ogre Tyrant

I dream that I am fleeing an angry mob. I am with the pope. We are in the burial chambers of the papacy. The room is filled with sarcophagi, each bearing the effigy of its owner. He takes his sword and thrusts it down into the carved stone face of one of his predecessors. We hear detractors coming at us from every corridor. There is no route out that is safe.

This dream reminds me of the catacombs in which I signed a prenuptial agreement twenty-one years ago against my will. I was pregnant at the time, and my mother was filled with such shame about my fall from grace that she demanded that I be married not only outside my home parish but in a church out of state. She did not want my disgrace to be witnessed by close family friends.

My fiancé and I complied and met with a priest who asked us to sign a document indicating that there was no "impediment" to the marriage. At that time, one of the impediments to marriage was pregnancy. I refused to sign the contract for obvious reasons.

The priest led me downstairs into the bowels of the church to meet with his superior. This corpulent monk sat across his desk from me in brown robes straining at the seams and told me that we could not marry unless I signed the paper. I asked him how I could possibly sign it knowing that I was pregnant. He told me that was not important. I was scared and humili- ated but also incredulous that the Church wanted me to lie for expediency's sake. I refused to sign.

In frustration the monk left the stone cell that was his office and told me to reconsider my decision. Within a few minutes my fiancé came into the cell and asked me to go along with the procedure so we could get out of this house of God with its rules and hypocrisy. I was appalled by his suggestion, because I thought he would rescue me and tell them to go away. Instead he joined forces with the priests. I caved in out of shame and weariness.

I am a different woman now. These ancient images of power and male authority no longer have a hold on me the way they used to. I take the sword from the pope and drive it deep into the face of this ancient stone figurehead. I no longer have to please, say yes, or go against my will. I now have other choices and the courage to exercise them.

To destroy the myth of inferiority a woman needs to carry her own sword of truth, sharpening her blade on the stone of discernment. Because so much of women's truth has been obscured by patriarchal myths, new forms, new styles, and a new language must be developed by women to express their knowledge. [6] A woman must find her own voice.

Strengthening her skills of communication helps the heroine to get along with different types of people. And having the courage to present her vision inspires other women to trust their images and words. The more we see women's art, hear women's poetry and plays, see dance works choreographed by women, and experience work environments designed by women, the more we will value woman's voice. As each woman dispels the myth of female inferiority, she becomes a role model for others.

A woman must claim her femininity as worthwhile. She must recognize her contribution to culture and society as intrinsically valuable in whatever feminine form: greater empathic skills in relationship, a strong and reliable aesthetic orientation, and an altruistic desire to provide care. Through this kind of self-regard, she is able to form an equal partnership with men and with her animus. The recognition that men are "male persons" without magic power or authority intrinsic to their gender is necessary for women to cease emulating men, needing approval by male institutions or belittling other women for their adaptations.[7]

The Myth of Romantic Love

In the myth of romantic love a woman is said to search for a father/lover/savior whom she thinks will solve all of her problems. She is prey to false notions of fulfillment: "If I find the right man I'll be happy." . . . "If I find the right boss I'll move up quickly in the ranks." . . . "If I'm with a powerful man, I'll have power too." . . . "I can help him with his career, business, writing." The unspoken message is, "I won't have to figure out what *I* want to do. I can live *his* life."

Men comply with the societal expectation that they take care of a woman and protect her from taking her own journey. "By promising to complete and protect her, they perpetuate the belief that she need not undertake a heroic journey. They will slay the dragons for her."[8] A man's sense of self is enhanced by rescuing a woman. The title of a recent lecture on the masculine principle, offered by the Analytical Psychology Club of Los Angeles, illustrates this well: "Knight in Shining Armor Seeks Damsel in Distress: Object Matrimony."

Women are waiters. Daddy's Little Girl waits by the window with her nose pushed up against the glass, peering into the darkness for the headlights of his car. In adolescence she waits by the phone anticipating the time when *he* will call. She waits for her first kiss . . . her first date . . . her first orgasm.

Women are trained into a state of expectancy. The next time we see our young woman she is a mother nursing her newborn infant as she waits for her husband to come home from work. He is her link to the outside world. He takes care of everything. She is waiting for life to begin. She has heard

the whispers: "You are not enough on your own." . . . "You
need completion." . . . "You need the other." . . . "You need
to wait."

In most fairy tales the heroine is taken out of her state of
waiting, her state of unconsciousness, and dramatically and
instantly transformed for the better. The catalyst for this
magical change is usually a man. Snow White, Cinderella,
Rapunzel, Sleeping Beauty, Eliza Doolittle, and Persephone
all share variations on the same prince! When the transformation of the heroine really occurs, however, it is usually the
result not of rescue from without but of strenuous growth and
development within, and over a long period of time.

Psyche and Eros

In the myth of Psyche and Eros, Psyche begins the story
under the spell of an illusory love and ends by achieving true
romantic love. Eros begins the relationship by rescuing Psyche
from a fate named death and then whisking her off to his
kingdom where all of her needs are attended to.[9] He tells her
not to concern herself about where they'll live or how they'll
eat; he'll take care of everything. In return he asks her not to
look at him at night or ask him where he spends his days.

Urged on by her sisters, who convince her that he is a
monster, Psyche challenges the myth of male supremacy,
defies Eros's orders, and lights her lamp to look at him as he
sleeps beside her at night. She spills some oil from the lamp
on him, and he awakens. At the same time she accidentally
pricks herself with one of his arrows and falls in love. When
she recognizes his divinity she tries to cling to him, but Eros
flees to his mother, Aphrodite. Psyche has disobeyed his
order, and he just can't put up with an impudent wife!

In *She: Understanding Feminine Psychology*, Robert Johnson likens
Psyche's desire to look upon Eros to a woman's challenge of
the authority of her inner male:

> A woman usually lives some time during her life under
> domination of the man within her or the god within her,
> the animus. Her own inner Eros keeps her, quite without

her conscious awareness, in paradise. She may not question; she may not have a real relationship with him; she is completely subject to his hidden domination. It is one of the great dramas in the interior life of a woman when she challenges the animus's supremacy and says, "I *will* look at you.[10]

When Eros leaves her, Psyche first tries to drown herself in her grief, but Pan suggests she pray to the god of love for help in her search for Eros. She goes to Aphrodite who, with great disdain, gives Psyche a series of trials of increasing difficulty.

Psyche first learns the task of discrimination; she sorts a huge pile of many different kinds of seeds. She then learns not to try to take elemental power directly into her own hands, as she attempts to pick golden fleece off low-hanging branches from a grove of trees frequented by dangerous rams. In her third task she learns how to order and set limits. By filling one crystal goblet with water from the center of the River Styx, she learns how to focus on one aspect of life at a time. In her fourth task, Psyche learns how to curb her generosity; she refuses to assist distractors on her way to the underworld. There she must obtain Persephone's beauty ointment for Aphrodite. She sets boundaries, says no, and also experiences failure to remind her that she is human. She must die to an old way of being before achieving wholeness.

Throughout her trials Psyche has assistance: ants help her sort the seeds, reeds tell her how to gather the golden fleece, an eagle fills the crystal goblet, and a tower gives her instructions for her underworld journey. Finally Eros wipes a deadly sleep off Psyche and takes her to Olympus to be made a goddess. Eros, the shape-shifter, is each one of her allies; he is her positive inner masculine guide.

Robert Johnson writes about the importance of a woman's inner male in the search for her autonomy: "Eros is a woman's animus who is being strengthened, healed, brought out of his boyish, trickster characteristics and made into a mature man worthy of being her mate. This is all done by her labors and his cooperation. He in turn redeems her."[11]

Eros and Psyche are married, and she gives birth to a girl

whom they name Pleasure. Psyche has been transformed through the endurance of her trials. She no longer lives under the spell of romantic love. Through her own hard work she has become a goddess. She marries Eros as an equal and achieves true love.

Many women who labor under the spell of illusory love want their spouse to be a demi-god who takes care of all their worldly concerns: mortgage, insurance, car payments, decisions about moves, and so on. Then they are blameless if he makes the wrong decision. The heroine must have the courage to demythologize her partner and take back responsibility for her own life. She must make hard decisions and earn her autonomy. When a woman is liberated or liberates herself from the belief that her fulfillment comes at the hands of a man, then she can find a partner who is an equal and enjoy true romantic love.

4

The Illusory Boon of Success

The Superwoman Mystique

During the road of trials a woman transcends the limits of her conditioning. It is a particularly harrowing time, an adventure fraught with fears, tears, and trauma. As a child and adolescent she is shaped to fit a role determined by expectations of parents, teachers, and friends. To move beyond them she must flee the captors of her conditioning, leave the Garden of Protection behind, and slay the dragon of her dependencies and self-doubts. It is a perilous journey.

If she first chooses the academic route, she'll have to make a decision early on about the focus of her studies. She is awarded her degree, but soon finds that a sheepskin is no guarantee for success. Everyone else out there is competing for the same position. She applies for graduate school or gets a job. She takes responsibility for herself and builds a new world around her based on her decisions and achievements.

If she chooses the world of work she begins to take steps to assure her advancement. She climbs the corporate ladder, becomes a middle manager, or starts her own business. She goes to conferences, takes exotic vacations, and becomes active in the community. She falls in love and gets married, but her husband does not define her self-worth. They rent a home with an option to buy and plan for their family. She has their children, continues to work, and juggles child care, groceries, and everyone's schedule. She is an assertive, independent, thinking woman. She enjoys the rewards of her efforts: money, a new car, clothes, and a title. She is on top of the world; she's having fun and is a force to be reckoned with.

Our heroine feels strong within herself, knows her capabilities, and has found the treasure of her seeking. If she has chosen the independent route she publishes her novel, mounts her exhibition, or outdistances the men in the two-hundred-meter race. She finds backing for her play, an office for her practice, or scales her first mountain. She has achieved the power, recognition, and success in the outer world that her mother only dreamed of. She has arrived.

Jill Barad, the thirty-nine-year-old executive at Mattel Toys, is one of only two percent of women who have been able to break through the "glass ceiling" into upper management. This achievement is a testament both to her own hard work and to the willingness of Mattel to have women in key positions. She directs a staff of five hundred employees and supervises Mattel's product lines from design to marketing.

In 1987 Barad was touted by *Business Week* as one of fifty executive women to watch as possible chief-executive-officer material. Meanwhile she balances demanding twelve-hour work days with a rich family life. She credits her "supportive family," which includes a husband willing to help shoulder the demands of child-rearing and a full-time housekeeper. But she has had to make sacrifices.

Once Barad walked into her son's third-grade classroom for a parent/teacher meeting and was greeted by her son's teacher, who exclaimed, "Oh, so Alexander really does have a mother!" "You feel awful," she admits, "but if you want to grow both parts of your life, there are times when you have to make concessions to both, and you just try to make the priorities the things that really matter. I don't think it's any different than what fathers have always been up against. The things you lose are moments to yourself, or for yourself, but you try to live with those priorities."[1]

Barad has had to set priorities that are still not fully accepted for and by women in this culture. Putting career before what others judge to be good mothering leads to the remark made by her son's teacher. Some women still envy and disparage another woman's success. No matter how successful she is, she still has to deal with the fact that the outer world is hostile to her choices.

Reaction to the Feminine Mystique

The superwoman cult of the 1980s promised young women that they could "have it all"—lucrative and personally fulfilling careers; loving, equal, and stable marriages; and joyous motherhood. Many of today's heroines became superwomen in reaction to the feminine mystique their mothers either endured or enjoyed in the 1950s. Because their mothers did not have the choice to compete in a man's world, nor the choice of whether or not to have children, these women became dependent on the men who supported them and the children they raised. The power they could not attain in the outer "male" world was compensated for by the power they wielded in the family.

Women who could not test their own skills and abilities in the male-defined world of remuneration grew to have unreasonable expectations of their husbands, sons, and daughters. What they could not achieve themselves they expected of their family. They controlled, cajoled, and manipulated regardless of others' feelings. In *The Second Stage* Betty Friedan writes about the tyranny of this maternal machismo:

> That control, that perfection demanded of home and children, that insistence that she always be right, was her version of machismo—her super virtuous equivalent of male strength and power, which she used to counter or

mask her vulnerability, her economic dependence, her denigration by society and denigration of herself. Lacking male power in society, which was the only power recognized then, she got her power in the family by manipulating and denying the feelings of men and children and her own real feelings behind that mask of superficial, sweet steely rightness. [2]

This mother could not express her loneliness, her abandonment, her sense of loss directly. All she could do was express her rage. This took the form of violent outbursts at her husband and children or a numbness induced by alcohol, food, or excessive spending. Her daughter watched and listened and heard: "Don't do what I did." . . . "Have a career." . . . "Live your own life." . . . "Women have no power." . . . "Wait to get married and have children until you know who you are."

These messages confused the daughter. Didn't her mother like being a woman, having a husband, and caring for children? Did the children ruin her life? Was being a woman awful? Would her life be ruined because *she* was female? Her mother's self-denigration and self-hate convinced the daughter not to be anything like her. She would be perfect instead. Friedan continues:

> I've noticed that women who feel least sure of themselves as women—in the shadow of their mothers' self-denigration, those mothers who didn't feel good enough about themselves to love a daughter strongly—are most likely to fall into the superwoman trap, trying to be Perfect Mothers, as their own were not, and also perfect on the job, in ways that men, grounded from boyhood in such games, don't try to be. That female machismo, passed on from mother to daughter, hides the same inadmissible self-hate, weakness, sense of powerlessness as machismo hides in men. [3]

Unfortunately, in an effort not to be anything like their mothers, many young women did become like men. They measured their self-esteem, their self-definition, and their self-worth against male standards of production. In the beginning

their successes were exhilarating. But the more they succeeded, the more demands were made on their time and
energy. Feminine values about relationship and caring took
second place to the achievement of goals. And many women
began to feel that they could never be "enough."

Peg is a successful architect in her mid-forties. She has been
designing industrial complexes for twelve years. She has children in their early teens, and her husband is supportive of her
work. She is financially successful and enjoys architecture but
feels that she is never enough. "No matter how hard I work
and how skilled I am, I always come up short. I work long
hours, I bring in new clients, my work is creative, but the way
the system is set up I can't win. When my father worked long
hours, he'd come home to a wife who prepared his meals and
took care of his clothes, his children, and his home. I don't
have a wife. My children get short-changed, my husband and
I have no time for sex, and I don't even know what it would be
like to have time for myself. I have the feeling that the only
way I can keep my career and have a family is to be two
people. I love my work and I love my family, but I want
someone to take care of me."

What many heroines want is exactly what their fathers
wanted and took for granted—someone to take care of them.
Someone loving and nurturing to listen to their woes, massage
their battle-weary bodies, appreciate their successes, and take
away the pain of their losses. They want a relationship to the
feminine. They want to let down, be cared for, and be accepted
for who they are, not for what they've done. There is enormous yearning for what feels to be "lost," but they know not
what is missing, so they fill the pain with more activity.

The Great Pretender

Our heroine has learned how to perform well, so when she
feels a sense of discomfort she tackles the next hurdle: a new
degree, a more prestigious position, a geographical move, a
sexual liaison, another child. She soothes her feeling of emptiness by massaging her ego with further acts of heroism and

achievement. She becomes enamored with the accolades winning brings. There is a great adrenalin rush associated with the achievement of a goal, and this "high" masks the deep-seated pain associated with not being enough. She hardly notices the let-down after her goal has been won; she is onto the next one.

This obsessive need to stay busy and productive keeps her from having to experience her growing sense of loss. But what is this loss? Surely she has achieved everything she has set out to do, but it has come at great sacrifice to her soul. Her relationship with her inner world is estranged.

The heroine's reaction to her mother's total dependence on husband and children for fulfillment has made her feel that she has to be more independent and more self-sufficient than any man in order to achieve anything at all. She will depend on no one. She drives herself relentlessly to the brink of exhaustion. She forgets how to say no, has to be all things to all people, and ignores her own need to be cared for and loved. She is out of control. Her relationship to her inner masculine has become distorted and tyrannical; he never lets her rest. She feels oppressed but doesn't understand the source of her victimization.

Joyce is an English literature professor in her mid-thirties. She has had a very successful academic career, teaching at a prestigious East Coast university. She is married to another college professor, a quiet, sensitive man with whom she shares a deep interest in the arts. Although their summers give them time to pursue other interests, Joyce always feels exhausted. She wants to have a child but feels that she couldn't handle another responsibility. After a series of dreams about a figure she calls the Great Pretender she begins to understand the source of her exhaustion.

"I have often wondered why I burn out before others. I get very excited about the idea of doing a conference, teaching a course, or leading a seminar, but it seems to me that I lack the required energy. There is almost an immediate resistance to doing what I say I want to do. I think it has something to do with being the Great Pretender.

"I have always appeared to be much older than my years. As a child, I was the great listener of my father, the great understander of my mother, the great caretaker of my brother and sisters. I knew how to say the right thing. I was wise for my age. I did well in school; my teachers loved me.

"I don't remember playing much during my childhood. I was too serious. I read a lot. My mother was always mad at my father for something, so I tried to put out the fires. He stayed away at work and pursued a career as a newspaperman. I tried to please by taking care of my mother and the children. My father wanted me to be strong, so I acted strong. I was really dependent, needy, and desirous of attention, but I did what he wanted me to do.

"I was carrying something that was too big for me to carry. I didn't learn the steps to be a hero, just how to pretend to be heroic. Now I get exhausted when anyone asks me to do something I don't want to do. Committees, conferences, articles all become an ordeal. I didn't have a choice as a young girl, so I resent it when I find myself in situations where I have no choice now. And when a male colleague starts to talk about the choices *he* had while growing up, I see red."

Joyce may no longer live with her parents, but her inner life is still controlled by her father. He continues to have a grip on her life energy. He still betrays her. He has become the inner male who continues to deny her needs and wants and who uses her for his own ends. She is exhausted at not having her needs met. She will have to liberate herself from this destructive father-image before she can relinquish the role of the Great Pretender.

A woman does not come to terms with betrayal by the father until she recognizes that all she has achieved has been based on pleasing the internalized father. In her desire to be responsive to this father-image she has developed a relationship to an inner male who does not always have her best interests at heart. He may be a critical, insistent driver who completely ignores her needs and wants.

Jung says that the creative process in a woman can never come to fruition if she is caught in an unconscious imitation of men or identifies with the inferior masculine in her unconscious. He defined the masculine as the ability to know one's goal and to do what is necessary to achieve it. If that inner masculine remains *unconscious* in a woman, he will persuade her that she has no need to explore her hidden motives and will urge her to a blind pursuit of her conscious goals, which of course liberates her from the hard and undramatic task of discovering her real individual point of view.[4]

The Myth of Never Being Enough

When the unconscious masculine takes over, a woman may feel that no matter what she does or how she does it, it is never enough. She never feels satisfied with completing a task because he always urges her to pursue another. Whatever she is engaged in in the present moment has no value; he urges her to think ahead. She feels assaulted and responds from a place of internal lack. "You're right, I should be doing something more; this is not enough." If I'm writing, my driver tells me I should be seeing more clients; if I'm seeing clients he says "get busy on the book."

There is a simple exercise to silence this inner tyrant and to train the heroine in the art of satisfaction. Divide a piece of paper into three columns. In the first column write something that you have done today, for example, "I weeded the garden." In the next column write "I am satisfied" and in the third column write "And that's enough!" It may sound simplistic, but after doing this exercise for a month or so you'll forget that you were ever "not enough."

One of the reasons women feel that they are never enough is because there are so many demands on their time and energy, particularly if they have young children. Time is a scarce commodity, and there are limits to a person's energy. But most women don't like to admit they have limits, and women have a hard time saying no. I encourage my clients to carry cue cards in their pockets to remind them of different ways of declining requests. It is also useful to keep these by the phone. "Thank you for offering me that position . . . I'll have to give it some thought." . . . "Thank you for the invitation . . . I can't accept it right now." . . . "Thank you for thinking of me . . . but I just have to say no." Women don't like to disappoint others, so they often give their assent with little thought about how it will affect their lives.

Most hero stories deal with the first half of life, when the hero builds an identity and establishes herself as someone in the world. This task involves going out into the world, acquiring skills, and achieving excellence. This becomes part of her identity. This work, whatever it may be, when consciously chosen is part of the "soul-making" process "which results in a personality that not only has more to give, but needs another person less compulsively."[5] This gives her confidence in her power to choose and to act and a sense of her own autonomy.

Women have to find autonomy before they can achieve wholeness. Examining the meaning of autonomy often involves discarding old ideas of success. Many women have sacrificed too much of their souls in the name of achievement. The rewards of the outer journey can be seductive, but at some point the heroine awakens and says no to the heroics of the ego. They have come at too high a price.

The heroine can say no to superwoman standards on the job or at home when she feels good enough about herself as a woman to acknowledge her human limitations. This may actually involve quitting a job and giving up power and prestige to *feel* again. Or she may decide that she doesn't have to have the cleanest house in the neighborhood and that her children and husband can begin to do their share.

Finding the inner boon of success requires the sacrifice of false notions of the heroic. When a woman can find the courage to be limited and to realize that she is enough exactly the way she is, then she discovers one of the true treasures of the heroine's journey. This woman can detach herself from the whims of the ego and touch into the deeper forces that are the source of her life. She can say, "I am not all things . . . and I am enough." She becomes real, open, vulnerable, and receptive to a true spiritual awakening.

5

Strong Women Can Say No

A strong woman is a woman who is straining.
A strong woman is a woman standing
on tiptoe and lifting a barbell
while trying to sing Boris Godunov.
A strong woman is a woman at work
cleaning out the cesspool of the ages,
and while she shovels, she talks about
how much she doesn't mind crying, it opens
the ducts of the eyes, and throwing up
develops the stomach muscles, and
she goes on shoveling with tears
in her nose.

A strong woman is a woman in whose head
a voice is repeating, I told you so,
ugly, bad girl, bitch, nag, shrill, witch,
ballbuster, nobody will ever love you back,
why aren't you feminine, why aren't
you soft, why aren't you quiet, why
    aren't you dead?

A strong woman is a woman determined
to do something others are determined
not be done. She is pushing up on the bottom
of a lead coffin lid. She is trying to raise
a manhole cover with her head, she is trying
to butt her way through a steel wall.
Her head hurts. People waiting for the hole
to be made say, hurry, you're so strong.

A strong woman is a woman bleeding
inside. A strong woman is a woman making
herself strong every morning while her teeth
loosen and her back throbs. Every baby,
a tooth, midwives used to say, and now
every battle a scar. A strong woman
is a mass of scar tissue that aches
when it rains and wounds that bleed
when you bump them and memories that get up
in the night and pace in boots to and fro.

A strong woman is a woman who craves love
like oxygen or she turns blue choking.
A strong woman is a woman who loves
strongly and weeps strongly and is strongly
terrified and has strong needs. A strong woman is strong
in words, in action, in connection, in feeling;
she is not strong as stone but as a wolf
suckling her young. Strength is not in her, but she
enacts it as the wind fills a sail.

What comforts her is others loving
her equally for the strength and for the weakness
from which it issues, lightning from a cloud.
Lightning stuns. In rain, the clouds disperse.
Only water of connection remains,
flowing through us. Strong is what we make
each other. Until we are all strong together,
a strong woman is a woman strongly afraid.

> Marge Piercy, "For Strong Women"

A Sense of Betrayal

For the past ten years I have listened to stories of women
between the ages of twenty-five and fifty-eight who have felt
that the successes won in the marketplace have taken a toll on
their health and emotional well-being far beyond the remuneration received for their work. Although they are satisfied with
the skills they have mastered, the independence they have
achieved, and the influence they now have in their chosen
field, there is a feeling of weariness and uncertainty about how
to continue. What is the next step?

There is not a desire to return to the safety of hearth and home, as advertised by *Good Housekeeping*, because for most women that could only be a fantasy. They are used to the satisfaction that work brings, and for most working women in the United States, their paycheck has become an economic necessity for themselves and their families.

The issue is not one of retreat; it is one of creating new choices. Many women today are taking stock of their situations and voicing a sense of betrayal. "What is all of this for? Why do I feel so empty? I've achieved every goal that I've set for myself, and there's still something missing. I feel somehow that I've sold out, that I've betrayed myself, that I've let go of some part of myself that I can't even name."

This feeling of being "out of sync" with oneself may be the first warning sign before a woman's body gives her a more concrete message. She may experience a difficult time recovering from the flu, develop insomnia, have stomach problems, find a lump in her breast, or start unscheduled bleeding. It may take a family transition such as a divorce, children leaving the nest, or the death of a loved one for a woman to fully awaken to a sense of spiritual loss; and she may not define it as such. She'll tell her friends and family that she just feels "off."

She has pushed so long and diligently along the heroic path that it surprises her that she cannot dismiss the feeling of missing something in her life. She does not understand the feelings of desolation nor of despair; these are certainly new emotions. "Sure, there were times when I felt 'down,' but I was able to work through them. All I needed was a new project, and I was up and running again. This is something different," says a forty-six-year-old development officer. "My doctor says there is no physiological reason for all the bleeding, but I can't help feeling that I am crying from the inside out." When women use the metaphor of being bled dry it is clear that they no longer feel fertile in their lives.

A forty-three-year-old nurse who works with infants of drug-addicted mothers says, "I long for the days when we all had young children and helped each other with child care, planned the children's birthday parties together, and listened to each other's frustrations. Now we're all so busy with our careers that we don't even have time for a cup of tea. We've lost a sense of community. I have no female network now beside the one at work, and all we talk about is how under-staffed we are and how to get the job done more efficiently. I really miss my women friends."

The sense of loss these women express is a yearning for the feminine, a longing for a sense of *home* within their own bodies and community. Most women today have spent their early and mid-adulthood developing and fine-tuning qualities that have always been considered masculine, including skills in logical, direct linear thinking, analyzing, and setting short-range goals. Women who brought emotions into the workplace were quickly told they did not belong there. Although many companies are now training upper management in a more feminine or "Beta-style" mode of leadership, which values feelings, intuition, and relationship, many women complain of under-valuing the feminine part of themselves.

"I miss using my hands to create; I haven't sewn in twenty years." . . . "I used to love to cook, but I don't really have the time for that now." . . . "My body yearns to kick off my shoes, sink my toes in the dirt, and run!" . . . "My bones actually hurt; it's not that I'm tired, I know what that feels like. This is new; they hurt for a connection with Mother Earth." These are the sounds of women who are beginning to feel a sense of dryness, a sense of sterility, a sense of spiritual aridity.

Fortunately, these women are able to express their feelings of loss. More serious are the scores of women who have what we define clinically as nervous breakdowns, blaming them-selves for not having the stamina, not being able to "take the stress" of the male-defined world. Many take refuge in alcohol or drugs to numb the pain of their loss. Or they are silent until the lump in their breast or cervical cancer makes them come to terms with the fact that the heroic journey did not take into account the limitations of their physical bodies and the yearnings of their spirit.

Spiritual Aridity

Women who burn out trying to fill male roles are scorched to their inner core. Marti Glenn, a psychologist from Santa Barbara, describes what happens when a woman's inner flame goes out: "A woman loses her 'inner fire' when she is not being fed, when the soul's flame is no longer fueled, when the promise of the dream held for so long dies. Old patterns no longer fit, the new way is not yet clear; there is darkness everywhere, and she cannot see or feel or taste or touch. Nothing means very much anymore, and she no longer knows who she *really* is."

She recounts her own experience while going through a period of burn-out in her career: "Last fall I began having a series of dreams of old women being put into body bags, carried, and rolled down a hill; dreams of me working and doing what I do best, leading workshops, having hundreds of people there. But on the other side there was a little girl crying and hiding behind a rock. I dreamed that I was asked by my boss to park cars, and that became my job. I got very good at parking cars. One dream after another had to do with the dying of the feminine. The other night I had a dream of women's skulls being crushed."[1]

Her inner child weeps and mourns the woman who is reduced to parking cars. A woman who gives her life over to the control of the unrelated masculine within becomes driven by the need to measure up and achieve according to male-defined standards. At some point she will come to realize that to survive and to live a healthy, satisfying life, she will have to make some changes. The assumptions she made about the rewards of the heroic journey have been wrong. Yes, she gained success, independence, and autonomy, but she may have lost a piece of her heart and soul in the process.

Such a woman will feel a betrayal by both the personal as well as the cultural mind that told her if she trusted goal-oriented masculine thinking she would be rewarded: be a "good" girl, and "father" will take care of you. She now feels utterly alone, deprived of comfort. To her the bottom has fallen out. There is a crack in her ordered world, a crack in the cosmic egg. A woman client describes it this way: "There is a thin shell surrounding me which is cracking. It is so thin that I can barely see it, but up until now it has kept everything in its place. I can feel it breaking, and I hear it. It is terrifying."

The world is not what she thought it would be; she has been betrayed. She rages against the loss of her cherished world-view and reluctantly realizes that she will have to move on by herself. Thus the heroine chooses not to be victim of forces beyond her control but to take her life into her own hands. Iphigenia was such a woman.

Betrayal by the Father: Iphigenia

Sometime during my early thirties I saw a film that portrayed the betrayal of Iphigenia by her father, Agamemnon. I was devastated by her blind trust in his love and his willingness to sacrifice her life in exchange for winds to speed his fleet to Troy. His mission there was to rescue Helen, the wife of his brother Menelaus. Iphigenia triumphed in the end by choosing her death and being redeemed by the goddess Artemis, but this was not part of the storyline of the movie, and I left the theater stunned.

Agamemnon and his brother Menelaus had assembled their fleets at Aulis to make ready for the invasion of Troy. A dead calm lay over the sea, and they could not sail. Their men grew impatient, and the seer Calchas, who was a Trojan traitor, told Agamemnon that he would never sail to Troy until he sacrificed his young daughter, Iphigenia, to appease the goddess Artemis for his boastful claims that he was a better shot than she. Agamemnon was bereft, torn between the love of his daughter and the allegiance he held to his brother, who had lost his wife to Paris of Troy, and to the men who were under his command and eager for battle and Trojan blood. Male pride had been violated, and a woman would have to sacrifice her life.

Agamemnon deceived Iphigenia by summoning her to Aulis with the promise of marriage to the noble warrior Achilles.

Iphigenia joyfully arrived at Aulis with her mother, Clytemnestra, to make preparations for the wedding ceremony. Clytemnestra soon discovered her husband's shameful deceit and begged him for mercy for their young daughter. Agamemnon refused, and Clytemnestra sought the aid of Achilles. Achilles, who was already married to Deidamia, agreed to help her because he too had been betrayed by Agamemnon. Unfortunately Calchas had spread news of the prophesy, and all the army was clamoring for the sacrifice of Iphigenia.

Agamemnon defended his betrayal to the enraged Clytemnestra and the tearful Iphigenia by saying: "I am no madman, nor have I ceased to love my children. This is a fearful thing, yet I must do it. Unless this sacrifice is made, Calchas swears we can never reach Troy: and all the Greeks are burning to smite the foe. If Paris goes unpunished for the theft of Helen, they believe that the Trojans will come to Greece and steal more women—steal their wives—steal you and our daughters. I do not bow to the will of Menelaus: it is not merely to bring back Helen that we go. But I do bow to the will of all Greece, and bow I must whether I will it or not—for Greece is greater far than any personal sorrow. We live for her, to guard her freedom."[2]

Clytemnestra was not swayed by this argument, and Achilles offered to fight single-handedly in the defense of Iphigenia, but the young maiden made her own decision about her life.

"I have chosen death," she said. "I choose honor. With me rests the freedom of our beloved land, the honor of our women through many years to come."[3]

Legend has it that at the moment the knife fell upon Iphigenia's breast and the fire was kindled, Artemis took pity on the young girl and snatched her away, substituting a doe in her place. After that the wind began to blow strongly from the west, and the fleet set sail for Troy. Tens of thousands of both Greek and Trojan young men fought to their death.

Iphigenia looked at the spiritual aridity of the male quest in its most fearsome form and lost her faith in her father. As she approached her death she was redeemed by the feminine principle (Artemis).

The betrayal of the feminine by the masculine has been recounted in endless stories and myths, but none as poignant as the betrayal of this daughter's love for her father with his promise of love and marriage to a heavenly youth. Iphigenia desired to give her father, Agamemnon, what he asked for. She sought his love, validation, and approval, but he betrayed her trust and sent her to her death. Her seemingly heroic act led to the downfall of a major culture and tragically affirmed the power, pride, and arrogance of the Grecian warrior quest.

Most women will do anything to please their fathers; they desperately want the attention of the male gods. Even if a man is aloof and judgmental, he still carries the power to determine how his daughter will function in relationship to him as well as to other men in the world. A woman who becomes aware of the continuing influence of this first masculine force in her life has a greater chance of dealing with her own blind allegiance to the masculine. She can say no. A friend of mine who is a Presbyterian minister describes an insight she had in working with a male boss very much like her father.

"About two years ago I began to realize that I was in a toxic environment. All of the programs I had instituted in the church were going well, but the more success I had, the more administrative and clerical jobs I was given. I began to think, 'have I come all of this way for this?' Each time I was promised a particular job, that promise was broken, and I began to feel that my gifts were being devalued. Sure I could do the job that I was given, but this was not what I was called to do when I entered the ministry. I felt tricked and betrayed by God. I began to lose my self-confidence, my energy, and my creativity, and I found that there was less and less of me that I could bring to the job. I was too busy at work to be nurtured by my spouse, friends, and family, and no one had time for the support group we had all promised ourselves when we left seminary. I also realized that the things that used to nurture me no longer did because I had grown; I was a different person.

"I had to examine not only what my personal issues were, but what issues accompany the role of a woman minister in a male-dominated Church. I knew that I had to work through my own questions so that I would not take them to the next congregation. I spent a year consciously addressing what 'father' issues became activated by working for an inaccessible boss, and I realized that I had done all that I could do within that particular system. I had done everything that was asked of me, and I was not feeling nourished in that job. I did not need to precipitate a crisis. I left before I got sick, with my integrity intact and with the programs I initiated running smoothly. But it did take me quite a while to work through the feeling of being betrayed by God." She chose to leave the system before it made her sick, knowing that she had completed both her personal business as well as her service to her congregation.

Betrayal by God

In *Laughter of Aphrodite* Carol Christ describes the roots of a woman's betrayal by God when she has grown up in or studied the "Father religions." In the years while studying the Hebrew Bible she sought approval from male professors. "I assumed that I could be the favored child of the Father if I figured out how to please him. It never occurred to me to question whether daughters could ever find an equal place in the house of the Father. Despite the pathological elements in my relationships with fathers, I did gain confidence in my own intelligence and abilities through their support. I gained a degree of freedom from traditional female roles by imagining a core of self that transcended femaleness. I assumed that the God whose words I would study transcended the genderized language of the Bible. I thought I could become like my male professors because we shared a common humanity, defined by our love for the intellectual life, our interest in religious questions."[4] Christ felt flattered to be told that she thought like a man, and she experienced contempt for women who were satisfied living out traditional women's roles. She felt special; she was a favored daughter.

She realized that this led to a betrayal of herself as a female.

Modeling herself on the Father and male mentors did not give her a clue as to how to think like a woman with a female body, or how to identify with other women, in recognition of her position as a woman in a patriarchal society.

Her relationship to the fathers changed in graduate school. In part it was because she moved from a coeducational university in the west to an eastern men's school. But it was also because she was no longer a promising undergraduate but a potential colleague-in-training, and because she began to try to visualize her future in more realistic ways. "In graduate school I found that I was viewed first as a woman by the men with whom I studied. The nonacceptance of me as a colleague was the catalyst that made me begin to question whether or not daughters could ever be accepted in the house of the fathers."[5] At this point Christ realized that she "needed to learn that [she] was not dependent on any Father or father for [her] sense of [her] own value as a person, as a woman, as a scholar, as a teacher."[6]

A forty-year-old woman raised in a Polish-American Catholic family grapples with the influence of the image of the Father in her life. She feels that she will never be enough because no matter what she does or how much she achieves, she will never be the "beloved Son, made in the image of God."

"I'm a figurative artist," she says, "and God has always been portrayed as a man. It might sound simplistic but for me God *is* a man. How can I ever be a peer with men if God is a man? I feel that the reason I get so stressed out is that I constantly fill my time with work because my image of myself as woman is so low. I am always trying to measure up to the "beloved Son."

Spiritual Daughters of the Patriarchy

For the last five thousand years culture has been largely defined by men who have had a production-oriented, power-over, dominating approach to life. Respect for life and for the limits and cycles of nature and her children has not been a priority.

"Men were big in ancient Egypt, big in Greece and Rome, big in the Middle Ages, big in the Renaissance. You only have to look at the history of art to see that men were once the measure of all things. Their physical proportions were ideal. Our notions of wisdom, justice, regularity and endurance were man-based, man-oriented, and man-regulated."[7]

For the last thirty years, women have been working in situations that for the most part are defined and run by men. Although women have made tremendous advances, and certainly not all men are dominating, the truth is that women have followed a masculine mode in most work situations—even most women bosses. Working long hours and focusing on profits to the exclusion of personal relationships is the rule, not the exception. When a woman begins to feel a sense of "what is all of this for?" she'd better not mention it to her boss or coworkers. Until very recently there have been few models for women who have chosen to say "stop, it's time for me to make some new choices." The women who are doing that now are traveling uncharted waters.

Pam is a client in her mid-thirties who has been a journalist for eight years. She has just left a prestigious, high-stress job with an entertainment trade magazine to free-lance and write a column. When I asked her how she felt about her decision Pam said, "No one at work realized how unhappy I was, so my boss was stunned when I said that I wanted to leave. The people I worked with didn't know who I was; I didn't feel safe. Being a reporter you can't reveal your feelings or opinions, so I wore a mask all the time. I didn't want to show my feelings or show who I was, because who I was someone who didn't want to be there. I never liked hard news: the pressure of squeezing people to say things they didn't want to divulge. I didn't like the constant maneuvering and manipulation.

"For six years I never listened to my own feelings," she continued. "Instead I acted out by being out of control with money. I was motivated by fears of failure; I didn't want to make any mistakes. Others' approval was really important to me, and I chose a career in the media where others' judgments are everything.

"I did find out, however, that I was a good writer and commentator. I was nurtured by my writing. Last year I had an opportunity to take a part-time job and work at home free-lancing, and a small voice inside me said, 'This is where I want to be, this is where I really want to be.' But I wouldn't listen to that voice. Instead I said, 'Tough luck, we're going forward.'

"This year I began to realize that I had achieved everything I set out to do. I was a good manager, I was a good writer, I was a critic that everyone read and quoted each week. I got a lot of attention. But I wasn't happy; I never listened to my feelings about not wanting to be there. I didn't want to be someone about whom my colleagues in the industry would say, 'She clutched.'

"And then I began to think about outer validation. Did I really want to be Howard Rosenberg, the critic at the *Los Angeles Times*? Yes, I could do it, but would I really *want* to? I don't like writing under deadline. I prefer doing free-lance pieces that I'm really interested in. I have to accept my own limitations; this is who I am. If I create the time to open up my creativity, I can write my ideas in a way that is funny and enjoyable to read.

"So I gave notice at work. I thought, 'I enjoy writing, and even if I don't make as much money as I'm used to and don't have as much prestige, I would have the joy and satisfaction of writing a column I love.' My boss told me, 'This is not the way it's done; you're making a U-turn, sacrificing your career.' That's a voice I've had to do battle with all my life, the governing voice that says, 'You should do it this way; this is the truth.' That type of absolute authority has always rankled me. But I listened to it for a long time.

"I quit my job and now I'm loving my work. I wrote a column last night that gave me so much fun and pleasure that I had to call my editor to read it to him. I was always waiting to be plucked from obscurity and made a star, but now I realize that I don't need to be. I can acknowledge myself on my own terms."

Pam had her ups and downs about her decision after she started her free-lance work, but within six months she had

Mistress of the Beasts

met her financial goal and was enjoying the diversity of assignments she was writing. Making a decision such as this takes a lot of courage.

What Happens When Women Say No?

When women say no to the governing voice inside that says "He's right, you are making a U-turn, sacrificing your career," a series of complex emotions are experienced at the same time. There is a feeling of emptiness, of somehow not measuring up by following the obvious career path to advancement. There is a fear of disappointing others, letting them down, destroying their image of who they think you are. But there is also a strength in saying no, in being self-protective, in listening to one's *authentic* voice, in silencing the inner tyrant.

I had that experience last spring. I sat in the Boulangerie, a neighborhood breakfast joint, listening to two grown men talk about the challenge that awaited me if I accepted an administrative job giving me the opportunity to be Joan of Arc, leading the troops to exhalted academic plains, toppling the heads of ineffectual faculty members with my sword, and sitting in the hallowed chambers of the king and his advisers. I came home feeling like I had just been invited into the Old Boys Club, although only to observe. I would never be one of them; they made that clear. They wanted me to take the job of administering the school, but I knew that the reins of power would still be in their hands.

There was something familiar about this; it was the same feeling I got while listening to my father talk to me about business deals: the feeling of being privy to some secret realm of power but not really an actor in the drama; the feeling of being an appendage, there to please, there to say yes, there to listen; an eerie feeling that if I took this job I would betray myself. I thought, "I don't like this feeling. Yes, I can do good work with the students and faculty, and it would be a great challenge, but the expense is not one I am willing to pay. I have finally carved out enough time to devote to my writing, and I want to follow that path to see where it takes me." I said no to their offer.

What was I left with? A sense both of deep mourning and of liberation. I mourned not fitting in, not producing as expected, not being part of a community I loved. But I also celebrated my newly won freedom from others' expectations and the knowledge that I had been true to my inner quest. Was I being selfish and fooling myself? I think not.

When the heroine says no to the next heroic task, there is extreme discomfort. The alternative seen to heroism is self-indulgence, passivity, and lack of importance. That spells death and despair in this culture; our culture supports the path of acquisition of position: more, better, faster. Most people fear that the opposite of this hubris is invisibility, and they don't know what to do.

When a woman stops *doing* she must learn how to simply *be*. Being is not a luxury; it is a discipline. The heroine must listen carefully to her true inner voice. That means silencing the other voices anxious to tell her what to do. She must be willing to hold the tension until the new form emerges. Anything less than that aborts growth, denies change, and reverses transformation. Being takes courage and demands sacrifice.

For the sacrifice to be complete, old ways have to be excised. Women have to start saying no to positions they really do not want to fill, even if it means a loss of acclaim from the outer world. And it usually does. It also leaves a gaping hole that needs to heal before the new way is clear.

While walking on the beach several days after making my decision, I had an image of a four- or five-month-old baby lying on her back kicking her feet. She was naked, lying in the sun, making gurgling sounds, and enjoying a freedom from constriction. It was a very healing image.

Saying No: The King Must Die

Women have a hard time saying no because it feels so good to be chosen, especially by the king. We enjoy pleasing daddy, our boss, our coworker, our lover. We don't want to disappoint others; so much of our self-image is invested in making other people happy. Our internal little girl doesn't want to be left out or left behind. It's too painful to choose not to join the fun. And we need the income.

In moving out of a state of spiritual daughterhood in which we serve male role models, there is rarely a Big Daddy saying, "You've done a good job. . . . It's just what I wanted. . . . Go ahead and make your own way." Instead the usual response is, "You're throwing away your career by not taking this position." . . . "How could you let us down?" . . . "You just don't know how to keep commitments." . . . "You're just not up to the challenge." These rebukes are difficult for anyone to hear but particularly trying for women who do not like to disappoint others or who have relied so much on males for approval and validation.

It is in these moments of being truly vulnerable, however, that we can really grow. Jean Shinoda Bolen says, "When we are doing something because it is expected of us or to please somebody else or because we are afraid of somebody else, we become further alienated from a sense of living authentically. If we just keep living out a role that we know well, the cost of that is to become increasingly cut off from that which is in the collective unconscious; that which not only nourishes us, but also provides the raw material that allows us to mess up. Very often in transition periods, that's exactly what is called for, a change by going through chaos, of losing the way, of being lost in the forest for some time before we get through and find our path again."[8]

What happens when we say no to the patriarchy? We have the time to create the space within ourselves to develop a *new* relationship to the masculine; not the masculine voice that has been split off from the feminine for centuries, as many men in our culture have been, but a creative masculine figure that leads us to the Great Mother, where we can heal our split from our own feminine nature. When we say no to the patriarchy we begin "our descent into the spirit of the goddess where the power and passion of the feminine has been dormant in the underworld—in exile for five thousand years."[9]

When I first started writing this chapter I began to have dreams about a positive inner masculine figure whom I called the "kitchen man" because I first encountered him sweeping a kitchen floor. He is a large bear-like man who is both gentle and solid. I have called upon his guidance several times during my writing when I anticipated moving into new territory. He is protective of me and moves at my pace, one step at a time. I have been surprised and energized each time I have called upon him and he has come. I had not expected this nurturing figure to be male. I have also been filled with a sense of wonder that this inner masculine figure is my guide to the Great Mother. In the passage below he takes me for a swim deep below the surface of unfamiliar waters. I write:

"Today I feel like I am in a state of in-between. I can feel the pressure of the waters pushing against my ears, blocking sound. We haven't yet moved deep enough, or maybe this is how it will feel. I have to remember to stay in the present. I am moving into new territory that I can't yet decipher. It takes staying in over my head. I see my words encased in others' words. Those are my words. I want to release them; what are they?

"We're down at the bottom of the ocean now, and I see many women floating in the warm, juicy waters. We are all being rocked by the rhythm of the sea. There's a spaciousness here, a sense of love. I look up through the cathedral of kelp, and I want to stay here forever. I hear the mother whales breathing with their calves in their birthing waters.

"The kitchen man and I swim together to a massive mammalian form. She sits on the bottom of the ocean floor; she is caterpillar-like and has many large breasts. (Diana of Ephesus) I suck from one of her tits but it gives water, not milk. I am surprised; it is nurturing. She smiles but she is detached; I feel no love for her or from her. She is very present, however, and very available. She is impersonal but she is *there*. I wonder about this to the kitchen man. He tells me:

" 'This is not a relationship with the personal mother, my dear; this is the Great Mother.' "

6

The Initiation and Descent
to the Goddess

they say you lurk here still, perhaps
in the depths of the earth or on
some sacred mountain, they say
you walk (still) among men, writing signs
in the air, in the sand, warning warning weaving
the crooked shape of our deliverance, anxious
not hasty. Careful. You step among cups, step out of
crystal, heal with the holy glow of your
dark eyes, they say you unveil
a green face in the jungle, wear blue
in the snows, attend on
births, dance on our dead, croon, fuck, embrace
our weariness, you lurk here still, mutter
in caves, warn, warn and weave
warp of our hope, link hands against
the evil in the stars, o rain
poison upon us, acid which eats clean
wake us like children from a nightmare, give the slip
to the devourers whom I cannot name
the metal men who walk
on all our substance, crushing flesh
to swamp

      Diane Di Prima, "Prayer to the Mothers"

Woman's Initiation

The descent is characterized as a journey to the underworld,
the dark night of the soul, the belly of the whale, the meeting

of the dark goddess, or simply as depression. It is usually precipitated by a life-changing loss. Experiencing the death of one's child, parent, or spouse with whom one's life and identity has been closely intertwined may mark the beginning of the journey to the underworld. Women often make their descent when a particular role, such as daughterhood, motherhood, lover, or spouse, comes to an end. A life-threatening illness or accident, the loss of self-confidence or livelihood, a geographical move, the inability to finish a degree, a confrontation with the grasp of an addiction, or a broken heart can open the space for dismemberment and descent.

This journey to the underworld is filled with confusion and grief, alienation and disillusion, rage and despair. A woman may feel naked and exposed, dry and brittle, or raw and turned inside-out. I felt this way while fighting advanced cervical dysplasia, during the dissolution of my marriage, and when I lost confidence in myself as an artist. Each time I had to face truths about myself and my world that I wished not to see. And each time I was chastened and cleansed by the fires of transformation.

In the underworld there is no sense of time; time is endless and you cannot rush your stay. There is no morning, day, or night. It is densely dark and unforgiving. This all-pervasive blackness is moist, cold, and bone-chilling. There are no easy answers in the underworld; there is no quick way out. Silence pervades when the wailing ceases. One is naked and walks on the bones of the dead.

To the outside world a woman who has begun her descent is preoccupied, sad, and inaccessible. Her tears often have no name but they are ever-present, whether she cries or not. She cannot be comforted; she feels abandoned. She forgets things; she chooses not to see friends. She curls up in a ball on the couch or refuses to come out of her room. She digs in the earth or walks in the woods. The mud and the trees become her companions. She enters a period of voluntary isolation, seen by her family and friends as a loss of her senses.

Several years ago, in the midst of a lecture on the heroine's journey that I was giving at Cal State Long Beach, a woman in the back of the lecture hall raised her hand and impatiently interrupted me when I mentioned voluntary isolation. "Voluntary isolation!" she cried out, "You've just named what I've been going through for the past nine months."

Everyone turned their heads to see a woman in her late forties rise from her chair with dignity. "Up until that time," she continued, "I was the owner and chief executive of a large design firm, pulling down over two hundred thousand dollars a year. One day I went into work and I just didn't know who I was anymore. I looked in the mirror and didn't recognize the woman looking back at me. I was very disoriented; I left work, went home, and never went back again.

"I spent the first month in my bedroom. My teenage sons and husband were terrified. They had never seen me like this before. I didn't even have the energy to get dressed in the morning. I couldn't shop for groceries, cook, or do laundry. I went into a period of what you call voluntary isolation."

Several women nodded their heads in recognition as she continued. "Now I garden. I've never gardened before in my life, but now it is the only thing I can do. I love the earth. My family is worried about me, they want me to go to a psychiatrist, to go back to work, to smile again. They miss my income. They think I'm crazy, but I don't even hear their words. I'm finding my way back to me in the earth every time I turn it over."

She had just spoken a truth that every woman who has made the descent knows. Women find their way back to themselves not by moving up and out into the light like men, but by moving down into the depths of the ground of their being. Her metaphor of digging the earth to find her way back to herself expresses woman's initiation process. The spiritual experience for women is one of moving more deeply into self rather than out of self.

Many women describe the need to remove themselves from the "male realm" during this period of voluntary isolation. Artist and therapist Patricia Reis writes:

> It took me four years to go through the whole process of destructuring, death, inner seeding, fruition, and re-

newal. One very important aspect of this time has to do with the fact that I removed myself completely from the whole outer arena of the "male world." In order to accomplish my own second birth, so to speak, I had consciously to separate myself from the world of men. It was this deliberate process of pulling in, or creating my own female matrix, that helped me to find my own inner powers, my own feminine ground. I doubt that I could have accomplished this in any other way. [1]

A woman moves down into the depths to reclaim the parts of herself that split off when she rejected the mother and shattered the mirror of the feminine. To make this journey a woman puts aside her fascination with the intellect and games of the cultural mind, and acquaints herself, perhaps for the first time, with *her* body, *her* emotions, *her* sexuality, *her* intuition, *her* images, *her* values, and *her* mind. This is what she finds in the depths.

I write with trepidation about the descent because I have great respect for the process and do not want to trivialize it. It is a sacred journey. In our culture, however, it is usually categorized as a depression which must be medicated and eliminated as quickly as possible. No one likes to be around someone who is depressed. If we chose, however, to honor the descent as sacred and as a necessary aspect of the quest to fully know ourselves, fewer women would lose their way in depression, alcohol, abusive relationships, or drugs. They could experience their feelings without shame, reveal their pain without apathy.

When a woman makes her descent she may feel stripped bare, dismembered, or devoured by rage. She experiences a loss of identity, a falling away of the perimeters of a known role, and the fear that accompanies loss. She may feel dried up, raw, and devoid of sexuality or experience the gut-wrenching pain of being turned inside-out. And she may spend a long time there in the dark, waiting while life goes on up above.

She may meet Ereshkigal, the ancient Sumerian goddess who hung her sister Inanna, goddess of heaven and earth, on a peg to rot and die. Every time a woman makes the descent she fears the dark goddess and what this part of her self will do to her. "I am afraid that she will grind me down, pulverize me, eat me up, and spit me out. I know that every time this happens I become more of myself than when I began, but it is an excruciating experience."

The descent is a compulsion; we all try to avoid it but at some point in our lives we journey to our depths. It is not a glamorous journey, but it invariably strengthens a woman and clarifies her sense of self. Some women today talk about their descent in terms of meeting the dark goddess in their dreams. They may experience the wrathful, devouring Hindu goddess Kali, filled with rage because of the original betrayal of her in ancient civilizations when her power and glory were turned over to male deities.

The *creatrix* principle of Kali and other female deities was usurped by the father gods. The biblical Yahweh, who called himself Father, made his children out of clay with his hands, copying the ancient magic of the Sumerian and Babylonian Mother Goddess, who had such titles as Nana, Ninhursag, and Mami.[2] "Hindus said there was a sea or ocean of blood at the beginning of the world; this ocean was the essence of Kali-Maya, the Creatress."[3] Egyptians called her Isis, the Oldest of the Old, who existed in the beginning of time. "She was the Goddess from whom all becoming arose."[4] The symbol of the feminine deity as the fertile creator of earth was eradicated during Christianity's successful attempt to eliminate the Mother archetype, replacing her with Father as Creator and Son as redeemer.[5]

Looking for the Lost Pieces of Myself

I prepare myself to meet her
Knowing not what to say
It has not been only men
who have betrayed her
I have betrayed her as well

I have been a father's daughter
rejecting my mother

I have always been afraid of
moving down into the darkness
I might lose
consciousness
I might lose
my voice
my vision
my equilibrium

How much of it is really mine?
My words are encased in others' language
My images are derivative of others' art
What *is* me?

I look for the lost pieces of myself. Somehow I feel that I
must find them before I meet her. What did I lose being a
father's daughter, trying to please and achieve? What did I
lose taking his side? I lost an element of truth, of seeing the
whole picture: the ugly, the crazy, the denied, the disappeared.

I look around and I see the blind heads of the mothers—
mine, my ex-husband's, my mother's best friend. Julia, Kathleen, Betty. What are they trying to say to me? "Pull us out
and reunite us with our bodies. Bury us properly. We have
been left here alone in the mud. We have no ability to move,
we cannot see."

"Take back the dark," they whisper.

What else lies buried with them? The ability to dream
dreams—my dreams, my fantasies. My imagination is somewhere here, strewn on this earthen floor; fairy tales and tree
houses and fantastical creatures I gather. Those are parts of
me that I take back. I reclaim them as mine. I take back the
feeling I once had that I could do anything I wanted to do,
bring anything I imaged into form. I knew it once and it was
magical. I used to sit by the side of the house and watch the
roses grow. I could be so *still*, I could feel life pulsing, smelling,
and sounding. I know the swamp; this isn't new. I've been here
before and have felt protected. The swamp, the woods: they
are my mother. I felt connected to the trees, to the mud, to

the grasses and leaves. I never felt alone. I take back that connection. It runs deep.

I sink down now into the strata. There are bones in the mud—white, beautiful, porcelain bones. I hold my own skeletal arms and ribs. The bones are the framework. I am excavating deeper and deeper for the lost parts of myself. I mourn them deeply. Where have they gone?

As I pick up these bones I see glimpses of the Mother Goddess under the earthen floor. She embraces a daughter. She is not whom I expected to see; she is not wrathful nor old nor ugly but a young woman with light brown hair. She soothes and embraces. She sits and listens and protects. She laughs and sings, her voice like bells.

But I am not there yet. I ask my guide to take me down.

He takes me down deeper than we have gone before, and I am truly afraid that I will drown. I sputter and swallow too much water as we descend below the swamp. He holds my hand and tells me not to be afraid. He leads me down into a cave. There I see a huge whale-like form encased by a scaffolding built by little Lilliputian men.

They are holding her down.

She can still move her enormous black tail. It swings back and forth in a strong, graceful rhythm. But the rest of her body is held motionless, spilling over the bars of this underwater holdfast. Nothing about her is menacing; I feel her deep sense of sadness. He brings me close to her, and I am terrified by her power.

"You can help me," she says. I pull back.

"No, I can't."

"Of course you can," she booms.

"By your presence they can no longer hold me. As each of my daughters comes to me of her own free will I am released."

As she says this the scaffolding falls away. The strength of the bars was illusory. Now she arches her back, and her mighty tail sends a tidal wave which undulates across the ocean floor. She swims and we swim with her. She loses her enormous size; she is no longer bloated and grotesque. She is

graceful and free. She moves through the water with the grace
of a mermaid. . . .

The Lilliputian men go on building their cage; somehow,
they have not realized that they hold her no more. We leave
the cave, and the waters change. They become warm and
milky. She stops and turns to face me, and she has long
beautiful golden hair.

"When my daughters come to me, not only are they healed,
but they release me from bondage," she says. She is the fish-
tailed Aphrodite-Mari, the Mother of the Sea. She is the Great
Fish who gave birth to the gods.

She no longer scares me. Like most women, this woman of
the depths is only frightening when her energy is shackled,
contained, and denied expression. When she can move freely,
all the creatures of earth and sea come to her. We are refreshed
and renewed in her presence. Women, and men too, have to
remember how to find her.

Mother/Daughter Mysteries

> The loss of the daughter to the mother, the mother to the
> daughter, is the essential female tragedy.
>   Adrienne Rich, *Of Woman Born*

I have always been very affected by the myth of Demeter,
Persephone, and Hecate. It touched me as a young woman
yearning for love, as a mother fiercely protective of my
children, and now as a woman in mid-life entering the years
of wisdom. From Barbara Walker's *The Woman's Encyclopedia of
Myths and Secrets* we learn about Demeter that

> Greek *meter* is "mother." *De* is the delta, or triangle, a
> female-genital sign known as "the leter of the vulva" in
> the Greek sacred alphabet, as in India it was the Yoni
> Yantra, or yantra of the vulva. . . . Thus, Demeter was
> what Asia called "the Doorway of the Mysterious Femi-
> nine . . . the root from which Heaven and Earth sprang."
> In Mycenae, one of Demeter's earliest cult centers, *tholos*
> tombs with their triangular doorways, short vaginal pas-

sages and round domes, represented the womb of the Goddess from which rebirth might come . . .

Like all the oldest forms of [Indo-European goddesses] she appeared as Virgin, Mother, and Crone, or Creator, Preserver, Destroyer. . . . Demeter's Virgin form was Kore, the Maiden, sometimes called her "daughter," as in the classical myth of the abduction of Kore, which divided the two aspects of the Goddess into two separate individuals. Demeter's Mother form had many names and titles, such as Despoena, "the Mistress"; Daeira, "the Goddess"; the Barley-Mother; the Wise One of Earth and Sea; or Pluto, "Abundance.". . .

The Crone phase of Demeter, Persephone-the-Destroyer, was identified with the Virgin in late myth, so the Maiden abducted into the underworld was sometimes Kore, sometimes Persephone.[6]

The worship of Demeter was well established at Mycenae in the thirteenth century B.C. and continued throughout Greece for approximately two thousand years, to then be replaced by the worship of Mithras and later of Christ. Her temple at Eleusis, one of the greatest shrines in Greece, became the center of an elaborate mystery-religion. Demeter was worshiped as "the Goddess" at Eleusis by Greek peasants throughout the Middle Ages, even up to the nineteenth century, when she was entitled Mistress of Earth and Sea.[7]

Early Christians were much opposed to the Eleusinian rites because of their overt sexuality, even though their goal was "regeneration and forgiveness of sins." Asterius said, "Is not Eleusis the scene of descent into the darkness, and of the solemn acts of intercourse between the hierophant and the priestess, alone together? Are not the torches extinguished, and does not the large, the numberless assembly of common people believe that their salvation lies in that which is being done by the two in the darkness?"[8]

In the darkness we are reborn.

The myth that became the basis for the Eleusinian Mysteries was described in the long Homeric "Hymn to Demeter,"[9] which details Demeter's response to the supposed abduction of Persephone by Zeus's brother Hades, god of the underworld.

Persephone was gathering flowers in a meadow with her companions, the motherless maidens Artemis and Athena. There she was attracted to an exceptionally beautiful narcissus with one hundred blossoms. When she reached out to pick it, the ground split open, and from deep within the earth, Hades came forth in his golden chariot pulled by black horses. He grabbed Persephone and took her to the underworld. She struggled against this abduction and screamed for help from her father Zeus, but he gave her no help. Hecate, goddess of the dark moon and of the crossroads, heard Persephone's cry from her cave.

Demeter also heard Persephone's cries and rushed to find her. Carrying burning torches, she searched for nine days and nine nights over land and sea for her abducted daughter. She never stopped to eat, sleep, or bathe in her frantic search. Many women feel like Demeter when they begin to look for the lost parts of themselves, when they experience dismemberment after having a child, separating from a love, or losing their mother.

At dawn on the tenth day, Hecate came to Demeter and told her that Persephone had been abducted. She had only heard but not *seen* who had abducted her. She suggested that they go together to Helios, God of the Sun, who told them that Hades had kidnapped Persephone and taken her to the underworld to be his unwilling bride. Furthermore, he said that the abduction and rape of Persephone had been sanctioned by Zeus, the brother of Hades. Helios told Demeter to stop weeping and accept what had happened.

Demeter was furious. She felt not only grief and rage but betrayal by her consort Zeus. She left Mt. Olympus, disguised herself as an old woman, and wandered unrecognized throughout the cities and countryside. While Demeter grieved there was no growth upon the land; it lay barren and bleak. When she reached Eleusis, she sat down near the well exhausted and mournful. The daughters of Celeus, the ruler of Eleusis, came to the well and were drawn to Demeter by her beauty and presence. When she told them she was looking for work as a nursemaid, they brought her home to their mother, Metanira, to take care of their baby brother, Demophoon.

Demeter fed the baby ambrosia and secretly held him in a fire, to make him immortal. One night Metanira saw what Demeter was doing and screamed in fear for her son. Demeter was furious. She rose to her full height, revealing her identity and divine beauty, and berated Metanira for her stupidity. Demeter's golden hair fell to her shoulders, and her presence filled the house with light and fragrance. Demeter remembered who she was.

Demeter commanded that a temple be built for her, and there she sat alone with her grief for Persephone. Demeter was the goddess of grain, so while she mourned nothing grew nor could be born on the earth. Famine spread, and the Olympian gods and goddesses received no offerings or sacrifices; finally Zeus took notice. First he sent his messenger, Iris, to implore Demeter to come back. When she refused, every Olympian deity came to her bearing gifts and honors. To each, the furious Demeter made it known that before anything would grow again she wanted Persephone back.

Zeus responded. He sent Hermes, messenger of the gods, to command Hades to send Persephone back to Demeter so that she would abandon her anger and restore growth and fertility on earth. On hearing that she was free to go, Persephone made ready to leave. But first Hades gave her pomegranate seeds, which in her haste to return she ate.

Hermes returned Persephone to Demeter, who was overjoyed to see her daughter. Persephone herself ran anxiously into her mother's arms; mother and maiden became one. Then Demeter asked Persephone whether or not she had eaten anything in the underworld. Persephone said that although she had eaten nothing in the underworld, in her excitement about returning to her mother, she had eaten the seed of Hades.

Demeter told her that had she not eaten she could stay with her mother always, but because she had eaten the seed, she would have to return to the underworld "for a third part of the circling year," during which time the world would lie fallow. The remainder of the year she could spend with Demeter, and the earth would bear fruit. After mother and daughter were reunited, Hecate came again and kissed Persephone many times, and from that day she was her "queenly comrade." Spring burst forth, and Demeter restored fertility and growth to the earth.[10]

In this myth we look at the three aspects of the feminine that are separated and then reunited: the Virgin/maiden, Persephone; the Great Mother, Demeter; and the Crone, Hecate. Persephone is pulled out of the innocence (unconsciousness) of everyday life into a deeper consciousness of self by Hades. She is initiated into the sexual mysteries and gives herself to Hades, becoming his consort. She loses her maidenhood, her virginity, her in-one-selfness, which Esther Harding calls "the essence of virginity." She becomes Queen of the Underworld. "The moment of breakthrough for a woman is always symbolically a rape—a necessity—something which takes hold with overmastering power and brooks no resistance."[11]

Persephone is pulled away from herself as her mother's daughter and enters the depths of her soul. This may be a universal experience for woman: losing a former sense of self and feeling lost, confused, and in the depths of depression, only to discover that in these depths is a new sense of self. Breakdown becomes breakthrough. "The Persephone of the Eleusinian rites who is Hades' bride, enables us to confront the most formidable moments of our lives as integral to them, as occasions for a deep see-ing."[12]

Finding her new sense of self, Persephone has no intention of going back to the status quo, regressing to identification with her mother again. So she swallows the pomegranate seed and assimilates the experience of the depths. "She has eaten the food of Hades, has taken the seed of the dark into herself and can now give birth to her own new personality. So also can her mother."[13] Persephone becomes a mother herself, who in turn has a daughter who dies to her and then is reborn.

"Every mother contains her daughter in herself and every daughter her mother—every woman extends backward into her mother and forward into her daughter."[14]

When Persephone is abducted, Demeter is overcome with grief and surrenders to her sorrow; she doesn't eat, drink, or sleep for nine days and nine nights (the symbolic nine of pregnancy). The loss of the daughter is the loss of the young and carefree part of oneself. It is a time of changing focus: from the exterior world with its outer projections to the inward journey and the work of the second half of life.

The Grain Goddess

I experienced the inconsolable grief of Demeter when my daughter, Heather, left for college. Without her I felt dead. I not only felt the loss of joy that I took in her daily presence, but I experienced viscerally the death of myself as mother. Like Hecate, who "is the goddess of the dark moon, of the mediumistic intuition in woman of that which hears in the dark but does not see or understand,"[15] I could not *understand* the reason for the depth of my pain. I had grieved when Brendan, my son, had departed for college two years earlier, but this time it was different. And much more extreme. I didn't sleep for two months after her departure, and although I continued to work, I cried every time I looked at her empty room. I wanted her back; I wanted things to be as they had been when we sang and joked and shared the events of the day. I even wanted her there to pick on me!

Helen Luke addresses the immense difference between the mother/son and mother/daughter experience: "On the archetypal level the son carries for the mother the image of her inner quest, but the daughter is the extension of her very self, carrying her back into the past and her own youth and forward to the promise of her own rebirth into a new personality, into the awareness of the Self."[16] Before experiencing a rebirth, I felt the chill cold of death.

At this time I had a dream in which troops with whom I had been traveling left me in a mountaintop cave at nightfall. It was snowing, and they had to get off the mountain while it was still light. They left me there because I had been wounded. The captain of the regiment gave me his glove as he left.

The next morning I reflected on the dream to find out what my unconscious was telling me. In my imagination I went back into the dream cave to see what was there for me to learn. I wrote:

"I look around, and there are ritual objects in the cave: a knife, an empty bird's nest, three stones, an empty holster, a canteen of water, and food rations. There is also a bedroll upon which I sit. My right thigh is wounded, and there is blood on my pants. It is cold out, yet I feel a sense of peace amid my fear. I have the ability to make fire. I eat my beef jerky.

"I know that I have the strength to stay here for three days; they will come back for me after that. The captain is my friend; I can count on him. Yet I feel immense fear. I find a bird's nest. It is rare to find a new bird's nest in a cave at this altitude. The nest is fragile. I feel that way inside too, but on the outside I must be a brave soldier.

"The objects in this cave are the playthings of a boy: the ally objects I once had as a young girl in the woods. The loneliness I feel now is the loneliness and bleakness of that time, before there were companions, before Heather and Brendan. They have been my life companions, and now they are gone. There is no one to play with; I return to the empty nest.

"I don't want to be alone; I don't want to be in the cave anymore. I want my children back, I want my youth back, I want my companions back. But it can't be that way anymore. I have to move on. I have to get up out of this cave and climb down the hill, even if it means my life."

Being a mother had defined a large part of what I was supposed to do with my life. Relinquishing that role left a gaping hole. I hadn't realized that I had made mothering my heroic quest. Before that, I had functioned in reaction to my mother—her frustration and her anger—in search of the approval of my father, church, school, or work.

"Now I feel naked," I wrote. "I no longer have the 'perfect mother' role as camouflage. And I have neither the energy nor the enthusiasm to be the 'perfect' therapist, writer, or artist. I just want to be an ordinary human being: no heroics, just a quiet inner quest. I have a knife, water, three stones, a bird's nest, food, and a bedroll. I know that I can survive; I don't have to depend on parents, children, or my partner. I can express my soul."

Like Demeter, I was able in time to move beyond my personal loss, but it took an amount of time that I judged unreasonable. I did not realize during my sorrow and grief that I was in the grip of the Demeter archetype. Shortly after I had this dream, Heather came home from college for a weekend stay at Halloween. She had been having a difficult first semester as well; she missed home terribly and had not yet found a group of friends with whom she could feel comfortable. Also at this time, I had been asked to submit an art piece for an exhibition entitled "Smaller Than a Breadbox." I asked Heather to help me paint the cardboard breadbox that had been supplied to all artists as a starting point for the theme. We started painting various designs together, and for some reason I started to paint grain goddesses. Heather asked me why the goddess I was painting had a tear falling from her eye. Without thinking I replied that her heart was broken, and I burst into tears.

It was only after this experience that I connected the grain goddesses we both painted to Demeter and the loss of my daughter to Persephone. I kept dreaming and writing and going through the ordinary activities of each day without enthusiasm. But I started to sleep through the night. "When it is time for a transformation of the whole personality, the birth of a totally new attitude, everything dries up inwardly and outwardly and life becomes more and more sterile until the *conscious mind* is forced to recognize the gravity of the situation, is compelled to accept the validity of the unconscious."[17] I was finally able to move out of my sadness about separating from Heather and realize that I now had work to do to find my daughter within.

The Descent of Inanna

Inanna, Queen of the Great Above, set her heart on
Earth's deepest ground. Turning her back on Heaven, She
stepped down. "But your safety?" anxious voices cried after
her. "If I do not return, go to the Fathers," She called
back, already at the first gate. "On my way to the funeral," She explained to the gatekeeper and the sandstone
bars gaveway. Then down She went—through mud that
tore the gold from her ears. Down through granite arms
that ripped the shirt from her breast. Down through fire
that singed the hair from her head. Down through iron
She thought was core that took her limbs. Farther and
farther down She hurled through emptiness that drank her
blood. Until at last She stood eye to eye with Ereshkigal,
Queen of the Great Below. That unpitying Eye froze her
heart and dazed She stepped through its pupil ringed with
skulls that chewed the flesh from her bones, as farther and
farther She fell in the hollow Abyss.

Janine Canan, "Inanna's Descent,"
in *Her Magnificent Body*

When we recognize our spiritual daughterhood in the patriarchy we have some excavation to do. We have to reclaim the
parts of ourselves that were ours before we cloaked ourselves
in the vestments of the culture. Sylvia Brinton Perera, in her
brilliant book *Descent to the Goddess*, uses an ancient Sumerian
poem about Inanna and Ereshkigal to look at the dismemberment that occurs when a woman sheds her identification with
and defense against the masculine, dies to an old way of being,
and waits for rebirth. [18]

Inanna, the ancient Sumerian goddess of heaven and earth,
descends to the underworld to witness the funeral rites of
Gugalanna, husband of her sister Ereshkigal, Queen of the
Underworld.

Before abandoning heaven and earth, Inanna instructs Ninshubur, her faithful servant, to appeal to the father gods, Enlil,
Nanna, and Enki, for help in securing her release if she does
not return within three days. She begins her descent. At the
first gate to the nether world, Inanna is stopped and asked to

declare herself. The gatekeeper, Neti, informs Ereshkigal, Queen of the Great Below, that Inanna asks for admission to the "land of no return" to witness the funeral of Gugalanna. When Ereshkigal hears this, she slaps her thigh and bites her lip and then instructs Neti to treat Inanna according to the same laws and rites as for anyone entering her kingdom. She must remove her royal garments and enter the underworld bowed low.

The gatekeeper follows orders and removes one piece of Inanna's magnificent regalia at each of the seven gates. She is stripped bare and judged at each of the seven gates. Ereshkigal fixes her with the eye of death. She speaks the word of wrath against Inanna, strikes her dead, and hangs her corpse on a peg to rot. When Inanna fails to return after three days, Ninshubur begins to lament and, beating her drum, circles the houses of the gods. She goes to Enlil, the highest god of sky and earth, and to Nanna, the moon god and Inanna's father, but both refuse to meddle in the ways of the underworld. Finally Enki, the god of waters and wisdom, hears Ninshubur's plea and grieves for Inanna.

He sets about rescuing her, making two creatures, neither male nor female, from the dirt under his fingernail. He gives them food and drink to bring to the underworld and tells them to grieve with Ereshkigal. They slip unnoticed into the nether world and comfort Ereshkigal who is groaning over her dead consort or moaning with her own birth pangs. She is so grateful for empathy that she offers them a gift. They ask for Inanna's corpse over which they sprinkle food and the water of life. Restored to life, Inanna is reminded that if she wishes to return from the underworld she has to provide a substitute to take her place. As she returns through the seven gates and reclaims her royal garments, demons cling to her so that they might retrieve her scapegoat.

The last part of the myth involves the search for her substitute, her consort Dumuzi, who did not mourn her death but took over her throne instead.

Inanna provides a pattern of feminine wholeness beyond that of the mother: she is the embodiment of the earth's fertility; goddess of the morning and evening star; goddess of war; goddess of sexual love, healing, emotions, and song. She is a wanderer; she broaches the taboo against crossing the threshold to the underworld. At each of the seven gates she relinquishes aspects of her identity. This "unveiling suggests the removal of old illusions and false identities that may have served in the upper world but count for nothing in the Netherworld."[19]

Ereshkigal was raped by the gods and exiled to the underworld, like all things having to do with nature and the body. She is the part of the feminine that has gone underground. She embodies rage, greed, and fear of loss. She is raw, primal, sexual energy; she is feminine power split off from consciousness. She is woman's instincts and intuition ignored and derided. "She is the place where potential life lies motionless, in the pangs of birth" before expression.[20]

I hold Ereshkigal in awe because I know that she has the power to scrape me to my very essence. Her impersonal force is not only destructive but transformative, "like decay and gestation, which work upon the passive, stuck recipient even invasively and against her own will. Such impersonal forces devour and destroy, incubate and bring to birth, with an implacable pitilessness."[21]

She is the place both of death and of new life lying dormant, the point of necessary destruction and of healing. In meeting Ereshkigal a woman confronts her own dark side, the rage and fury left unexpressed for decades while she tried to please the fathers above. A woman client describes this as the ball of molten iron that sits in a depression, eating away her chest.

Ereshkigal represents a woman's relationship to the workings of the deep layers of her psyche, her body, her instinctive nature. She demands reverence and respect. She looks upon us with her eye of death, seeing what we ourselves do not want to see. She demands that we look at those parts of ourselves from which we have split.

At her most negative she can bring all life to a standstill. A client describes how her mother looked through her with an "evil eye": "Whenever she was mad at me, she would fix me with her evil eye of hate and go into silence for a week. It was like a black hole. She acted as if I were dead; she didn't see me, hear me, talk to me. I was bereft at being so utterly separated from her; I felt that life had ended and I couldn't go on. I pleaded with her to stop, but she never gave in."

Ereshkigal impales Inanna on her peg, filling her "all-receptive emptiness of the feminine with feminine yang strength. It gives a woman her own wholeness, so that the woman is not merely dependent on man or child, but can be unto herself as a full and separate individual."[22] She knows what she wants to say yes and no to. When a woman begins to assert herself, she is often seen as disagreeable, ugly, and a bitch, as no longer willing to smile, swallow feelings, numb out, and please. But for a woman to be whole, she must reclaim the dark mother in herself.

Meeting the Dark Mother

During the descent, a woman experiences a period of introversion or depression, a slow painful self-pregnancy in which she scrapes away her identification with ego-consciousness and goes back to a state of body/mind knowing before there were words. She may feel an incredible sense of emptiness, of being left out, shunned, left behind, without value. She may feel homeless, orphaned, in a place of in-between. Like both Demeter and Inanna, she will bear no fruit, no product. She may feel naked and exposed, sexless, arid, and raw. She may dream images of tunnels, subways, wombs, tombs, being swallowed by snakes, or finding herself like Jonah in the belly of the whale. If she can allow the descent to be a mindful initiation, she need not become lost in the dark.

A client dreams of meeting the dark mother in an underground train. "I am on a subway with my five-year-old daughter, another child, and my husband. The train comes into the station and we start to get off. My daughter, Maraya, runs off first, and her hat blows off behind the train and she runs after it. I run after her and don't see her, but I see kids on the other side of the tracks running after something. I can't see Maraya, but I know she is alright; she hasn't fallen down onto the tracks. I rush back into the subway car to get my luggage, camera bag, purse, and hand them out to my husband. When I go back for more the train takes off. I'm on the train with no luggage, no money, no camera, and I don't know the name of the station where I left my family. There are only two other women in the subway car. One is reclining as if ill, and the other is attending her. I ask them the name of the station we have just left; they don't know, but they say we have at least another forty minutes to the next stop. I start to tell them my dilemma, and they say, 'You really are in a fix, aren't you?' But they don't offer help. I think, I'll have to ask them for at least one dollar to get back, but I don't know the subways or if my family will wait there for me."

I ask her to converse with the women in the subway car. "They are my mother and me. 'What are you doing on the train with me?' I ask. They tell me, 'You have to face us before you can get off.' I face them. The mother-reclining figure has the power; the daughter attends her. The mother is derisive, lazy, commanding. I shrink in her presence but attend to her lovingly. I would like to kill her.

"She is sickly and dependent; her power is in her dependence. She keeps me chained to her with her dependence. I feel numb; I don't even know where this train goes. The destination is unknown, but I feel trapped in this car with her. I want to tell her to get up and walk, but I am afraid that she will punish me by withdrawing her dependence. She doesn't really love me; I know that, yet I pretend she needs me. I pretend and become the long-suffering martyr. Aren't I good? I take care of my mother.

"I need to get up at the next station and walk away from her. It would be so liberating. That woman across from me is so free. She has nothing. No baggage, no family, no money. She is boundless even though she is afraid. I am tied to something that is not even there: an old identity, the daughter of an ill mother, proving myself worthy. Meek and silent, what would happen if I got up and walked away? I would lose my mother. I would lose my image of serving my mother. I would no longer be in the service of the negative mother. I would break through the complex.

"I can't continue to serve and to breathe. I want to see the light of day. If she wants to stay in the subway that is her journey. I want to breathe fresh air. She shrivels up as I tell her I will leave the train when it comes into the station."

This woman spent the next forty days in bed with pneumonia; she ran a mysterious fever which kept her in a constant sweat. It was a time of suffering and isolation, but also a time of purification and transformation. She realized that she no longer had to suffocate with rage for her mother. She had read the myth of Inanna and Ereshkigal, and one day toward the end of her illness she came into therapy and said that she had forgotten to tell Ninshubur that she was "going under."

Mindful Suffering and Return

After three days Inanna does not return from the underworld and her trusted assistant, Ninshubur, appeals to the sky and moon gods for help. Like many women, Inanna "looks for love in all the wrong places"; she looks to the fathers, who seemingly have all the power but who are neither capable nor generous enough to help. This is a recurring theme for myself and for many daughters of the patriarchy who expect help and approval from those who refuse to see them as they are. Women have to learn where their true source of validation is.

Ninshubur goes to Enki, the wily water and wisdom god, ruler of the flow of seas and rivers. He is the generative, creative, playful, empathetic masculine. [23] With the dirt or clay under his fingernails, he improvises what the moment needs. He creates creatures that are neither male nor female to embody humility, empathy, and the ability to mirror Ereshkigal's feelings. [24] She is in deep mourning, and these asexual creatures suffer with her, inside and out. They don't implore her to *do* anything; they simply allow her to *be* in her pain. They sing her lamentations with her. Ereshkigal feels heard, and this allows the deep feminine to "accept her pain as it is— as part of life's natural process." She doesn't have to blame

anyone; she can simply be with the suffering and heal natu-
rally.

This quality of empathy or *being with* the pain helps one to
move through it. It also prevents what I refer to as "premature
ejaculation"—moving to action too soon because the pain of
holding the tension of the unknown is unbearable. If we have
the patience to allow the process its full due, deep healing can
occur. If we abort our process we never allow ourselves to
come to full term. Women and men need to support each
other to honor the feminine cycle, which, like the cycles of
life in nature, is one of death, decay, gestation, and rebirth.

When Ereshkigal feels heard, she allows the sexless creatures (the *kalaturra* and *kurgarra*) to restore Inanna to life.
Inanna feels the stirrings of life within her. She is revived with
food and water and slowly comes to herself, making the return
from the underworld to seek her substitute. She has met the
dark goddess and knows that "all change and life demand
sacrifice. That is exactly the knowledge that patriarchal moral-
ity and the fathers' eternally maiden daughters have fled from,
wanting to do things right in order to avoid the pain of bearing
their own renewal, their own separate being and uniqueness."[25]

When Inanna returns from the underworld she is not all
sweetness and light; just as when a woman comes out of
voluntary isolation to assert herself, it is often not a pretty
sight. Beware family and friends that want her to go back to
the way she was before. She now realizes the extent to which
she has sacrificed herself in pleasing others, and she is not
willing to do things the old way. She ruthlessly cuts away
people and situations that do not support who she has become.

Inanna finds Dumuzi, her consort, her equal, sitting on her
throne, unconcerned about her plight. She confronts him and
commands that he be taken away to the underworld. She
sacrifices the one most cherished to her. "The beloved Dumuzi
here is the favorite animus attitude, the old king, that the
feminine soul must render to the Self, kill as the primary
source of her own validation and identity."[26] In other words,
he is that part to which we look for approval. I have listened

to many women clients who, during the writing of their doctoral dissertations, came to the realization that the only reason they had embarked on that particular rite of passage was to get the approval of the fathers. At that point many chose to become A.B.D.s (all-but-dissertations) instead of Ph.D.s.

The goddess Inanna mourns the loss of her love, and it is then that Inanna is heard by a human woman. Geshtinanna, the sister of Dumuzi, is herself grieving the loss of her brother. Out of love and grief she appeals to Inanna to take herself instead of Dumuzi. Inanna is so moved by her offer of conscious sacrifice that she allows Geshtinanna to share Dumuzi's time in the underworld; each would spend six months in the underworld and six months on earth. [27]

Geshtinanna is the new feminine; she is a wise woman who is in touch with her feelings, humble, and *conscious of her sacrifice.* She is willing to endure the cycle of descent-ascent-descent; she is related to her own masculine nature as well as to the depths of her feminine. She is "a model of one who is willing to suffer humanly, personally, the full spectrum that is the goddess."[28] She ends the pattern of scapegoating by choosing to confront the underworld herself.[29] She blames no one.

Geshtinanna has much to teach the modern-day heroine; she makes her descent not for accolades and approval but to experience the full cycle of her feminine nature. She gains the wisdom of the cycles of change, accepting the dark, instinctive side which helps us find meaning in suffering and death as well as the light, joyous side which reaffirms our strength, courage, and life.

7

Urgent Yearning to Reconnect with the Feminine

The Worm Baby

I dream that I have a baby. She is very small, almost like a pale worm. Lucien and I are out walking along Main Street, and all of a sudden I remember the baby. We rush home and find her outside, in a stroller on the front porch step. I take her out of the stroller and she is famished. I am about to offer her my breast when I realize I have to change her first. I say to Lucien, "You have to develop a relationship with her by talking to her." I change her, and she looks so pitiful, so small. She can hardly cry; she just makes a small cat-like sound. She is not demanding, just sad. I am worried for her survival because I didn't even remember that I had her. Milk comes into my left breast as she cries.

When I reflect on this dream, the image of the worm baby reminds me of the unmasked Darth Vader in George Lucas's *Return of the Jedi*. Luke Skywalker removes his father's mask and is shocked and saddened to see the undeveloped head of the warrior king. In serving the state, he had not developed his humanity. When I take off the mask of my father, I see a sad little boy wanting to be held, stroked, and told that he is loved just as he is. As I unmask the father within myself, the heroic aspect, I see my deep feminine nature that yearns to be acknowledged, talked with, cleansed, changed, and fed. But this connection is so fragile that at times I forget it. I certainly have enough milk to nurture this newborn feminine; I just have to remember.

When a woman has made the descent and severed her identity as a spiritual daughter of the patriarchy, there is an urgent yearning to reconnect with the feminine, whether that be the Goddess, the Mother, or her little girl within. There is a desire to develop those parts of herself that have gone underground while on the heroic quest: her body, her emotions, her spirit, her creative wisdom. It may be that a woman's relationship to the undeveloped parts of her own father gives her a clue to her true feminine nature.

If a woman has spent many years fine-tuning her intellect and her command of the material world while ignoring the subtleties of her bodily knowings, she may now be reminded that the body and spirit are one. If she has ignored her emotions while serving the needs of her family or community, she may now slowly begin to reclaim how she feels as a woman. The mysteries of the feminine realm will appear in her dreams; in synchronistic events; in her poetry, art, and dance.

Body/Spirit Split

Historically, the connection between body and soul was destroyed with the overthrow of the Mother Goddess. It is only now, with the threat of massive destruction of Mother Earth, that this connection is being reclaimed. When humankind forgot the sanctity of the earth and began to worship its gods in churches and cathedrals instead of in groves and on hilltops, it lost the sacred "I-Thou" relationship with nature. We forgot that we were her children, interconnected with all of her species. We lost the sense of sacredness embodied in all living beings, trees, rocks, oceans, four-leggeds, birds, children, men, and women. With this disregard for the sanctity of nature came the denial of the sanctity of the body.

It was not always this way. When the body of woman was the equivalent of the body of the Goddess, a woman was the container for the miracle of life.

In earlier times when metaphor and archetype rather than scientific knowledge described how things worked, there was a feeling of awesomeness toward women. The awesomeness had to do with the changes her body went through. A girl became a woman when she menstruated; blood has always had a numinous quality. She bled every month until she became pregnant, and then she stopped bleeding for nine months and became a container for new life. It was thought that she retained the blood in her body in order to make a baby. After she had the baby she would bleed once again, month in and month out, until menopause when once again she stopped bleeding. This was also considered awesome, for now it was thought that she retained the blood in her body not to make a baby but to make wisdom. Women are now reclaiming this very different way of looking at their experience, as they bring back into the world a sense of the sacredness of matter. [1]

During the Middle Ages, and particularly since the Industrial Revolution and its deification of the machine, the physical body of both women and men, like Mother Earth, has been sexually and physically abused. The body has been pushed beyond limits of strength and endurance and made to conform to cultural expectations of size, shape, and beauty in the interest of serving human greed. The denigration of the female body has been expressed in cultural and religious taboos surrounding menstruation, childbirth, and menopause; [2] it is also reflected in mounting statistics documenting rape, incest, and pornography. The sacredness of the female body, the recognition of sacredness in matter, was lost as people began to worship the father gods. The reverence and fertility once accorded a menstruating woman went underground along with the Goddess.

In her absence, some women forgot the deep wisdom of the female body and the mysteries of feminine sexuality. Women *know* with their bodies. Jean Shinoda Bolen says that "when we know something in our bodies as well as with our mind and hearts, then we know something deeply about ourselves, and it is this dimension that has been out of balance in our

Christian civilization and our Christian-influenced psychology. It has been so much a father psychology as well as a father theology, where mind, interpretations, and the word are the transformative experience, and that's not true [for women]."[3]

Female Sexuality

The loss of power associated with woman's sexuality has been a reality across cultures ever since man discovered that he had a role in the procreation of children. To protect patrilineal descent, men have for centuries tried to control women's sexuality. "Although man needs woman, he tries to keep her power under control, legislating against woman's free use of her sex in case she compromises the fragile but tenacious social structure of our patriarchal society.[4] To protect his patrilineal descent, his son must be the son of the father and not the son of the mother."[5]

Sheela-na-gig

Even in Celtic societies, where the descent of the child was matrilineal, woman's sexual power was considered dangerous, unhealthy, and frightening. Jean Markale recounts that when the Celtic Great Mother, Rhiannon, was pushed underground she took the form of the white boar or sow. In the following Welsh story told by Markale, it is clear that the sow goddess, Henwen, was feared, persecuted, and denigrated by Arthur and his men. The power of her fertility aroused great terror in their hearts.

It had been predicted that Britain would suffer at the hands of the children of Henwen (the Old White), so when it was found that she was pregnant, Arthur assembled the British army and set out to destroy her. She gave birth and, upon being pursued by her attackers, threw herself into the sea. Her young jumped in behind her. At Maes Gwenith ("Field of Wheat") in Gewent, she gave birth to a grain of wheat and a bee. At LLonyon in Pembroke, she birthed a grain of barley and a grain of wheat. At Riw-Gyverthwch in Arvon she gave birth to a baby wolf and a baby eagle. And at Llanveir she bore a cat which the swineherd threw from the rocks into the sea.[6] Wheat, barley, bees, and cats were all ancient symbols of the Goddess. The patriarchy may pursue her, but her progeny will continue to flourish.

The sow goddess embodied fertility and abundance in many ancient cultures. The pig was a symbol of the Goddess in Mesopotamia; in old Europe it gained significance through the cult of Demeter and Persephone because the Eleusinian rites evolved through vegetation ceremonies, which used the sacred pig. After the festivities were concluded, the women went off with the men and made love in the furrows of the field to ensure the success of the crops. This ritual establishes a direct connection between human sexuality and agricultural fertility.[7] Presumably, women's sexuality was accorded the honor and reverence it deserved for its ability to bring life on earth. Spirit and body were one.

Most women have lost that sense of power connected with their sexuality. Man has demeaned woman instead by calling her temptress, evil seductress, and devourer. The original power of the goddess's raw sexual and procreative energy has been seen as an enormous threat to masculine authority. It has also been perceived as counterproductive to our cultural work ethic. "The danger of free sexual relations, as symbolized in the goddess, Our Lady of the Night, lies in the possibility of their leading to total satisfaction of the instinctive desires of men and women, followed if not by sleep, then by a state of inertia, close to *nirvana*, in which all will to live disappears. To put it another way, there would be a general regressus ad uterum, a return to true paradise in the real or imaginary protection of an ever-damp and nourishing maternal womb."[8]

Ancient goddess figures that glorified female genitalia have for centuries been defaced by conquering tribes and Christian priests. The Sheela-na-gig, a Celtic symbol of the devouring mother aspect of the Goddess, was carved in stone on temples and castles all over Ireland and Britain. She featured "huge genitalia held apart with both hands and bent legs offering a fantasy of unlimited sexual license and at the same time a comic reminder of our origins. She expressed the intimate and awesome sight of the birth mystery and symbolized the moment when the bloody placenta is severed and new life is released."[9] In most of these remaining effigies the genitalia have been scraped off the stone, and the original visage is unrecognizable.

With such active destruction of symbols of feminine fertility, it is no wonder that some women today feel shame about their genitalia and develop sexual "dis-ease," such as condeloma, dysplasia, and herpes. They keep this secret from their family and friends for fear of being considered dirty. They compare the flower of their sexuality to others and find their labia and vagina lacking. Nothing is ever right with their bodies; adolescent girls decry the size of their hips and breasts instead of celebrating their ability to give birth and nurse their young. They make derogatory remarks about menstruation because they have never been told that having their period or "being on their moon," as Native Americans refer to menstruation, is a time of cleansing; a time of dreams, insights, and intuition; a time of enormous power to be reclaimed and respected.

Family Messages about the Female Body

"Tell me about being a woman," a thirty-five-year-old woman says. "I live inside a body that weighs over two hundred pounds, and I don't identify with being feminine at all. I know what it feels like to be a mother; I like to nurture children and my clients, but I don't identify with being a *sexual* woman. My parents always told me not to come home pregnant, and I guess I thought that if I had sex and got pregnant, I wouldn't be allowed home at all. So at thirteen I started putting on weight to protect myself. I remember being at a school dance in eighth grade, and the most popular boy came up to me and asked me to dance. I was so afraid of being touched by him that I told him he was too short. Right after that I started to eat."

Many women have so much difficulty living inside a female body that they abuse it with food, alcohol, drugs, overwork, or overexercise to exorcise the discomfort of being female. If a daughter has become male-identified in pleasing her father, she emphasizes the development of her mind and intellect and rejects her female body. She forgets how to listen to its wants and needs. The body is intelligent; it knows when it is hungry, thirsty, needs rest, wants to exercise, wants sex, doesn't want sex, and is out of balance. Many of us, however, have been trained to ignore and override communication from our bodies.

Women's bodies are public domain, as evidenced clearly at the present time by the furor over abortion. Everyone has an opinion about what a woman should or should not do with her body. When it comes to employment, many fathers implore their daughters to lose weight and keep up appearances so they can get good jobs as secretaries. These same daughters may have had their sights on management positions, where they would have power and status, but they are told to physically conform to what is appropriate for a woman in a support role. For years, women have been told that in business they can't do as good a job as men because they menstruate and give birth. It is no secret that in spite of the advances women have made in the last twenty years, they are still penalized for taking time off to have children and care for them as infants by being overlooked for promotions and salary increases.

If a woman's mother did not relate to her own body as female, or made disparaging remarks about her sexuality or the sexuality of other women, she was probably unable to cherish the female body of her baby daughter. [10] Some women tell their daughters horror stories about their first penetration or about the pains of childbirth, so many girls fear sexuality, loathe their bodies, and slowly cut themselves off from their instincts. If the "emphasis in a family was on perfect performance without any genuine recognition of the Becoming or Being of the child, she very early learned that instinctual responses were not acceptable; thus her anger, fear, even joy were driven into the musculature of her body, chronically locked in and inaccessible to everyday living. When authentic feeling is cut off from the instincts, genuine conflict either remains in the unconscious or becomes somatized there."[11]

The most obvious cause of a woman's separation from the feelings in her body is incest, rape, or physical abuse. When a girl is sexually abused by a male in authority—a father, brother, uncle, grandfather, family friend, teacher, doctor, cleric, or boss—she numbs her body to forget the humiliating pain associated with the sexual trauma. This pain does not disappear with its immediate cause, however. The experience is stored in her body at the place of the wounding, such as her lips, breasts, labia, vagina, or cervix, causing tightness, physical pain, confusing sensations of pleasure, numbness, or disease. I have found that many of my clients who experienced sexual abuse at an early age either become incredibly sensitive body-workers or are totally out of touch with their physical limitations. They either turn the wounding into an experience of deep understanding of how pain and confusion are locked in the body and can be released, or they armor their poor wounded body, anesthetizing themselves to their own instincts and intuition. They no longer trust their "gut" because listening to their body triggers unwanted memories and feelings.

As a woman returns from the descent, she takes back her body, and in this act of reclamation, she takes back not only *her* personal physical form but she embodies the sacredness of the feminine for all of us. She begins to make conscious its needs. Through conscious nutrition, exercise, bathing, rest-taking, healing, lovemaking, birthing, and dying she reminds us of the sanctity of the feminine. For many women, including myself, the most sacred moments have been physical ones: being held, making love, nursing a child. Nothing brought me closer to the ecstasy of the sacred than giving birth. The sacred dimention *is* embodied, and the soul of a human being as well as the soul of a culture cannot evolve if the body is not reclaimed and honored.

When I think of women who bring the sacred aspect of the female body into their work and lives, I recall Arisika Razak, a midwife from Oakland, California, who created the "vulva dance" to honor woman's sexuality.

"As a midwife," she says, "I spend a fair amount of time focused on women's genitals, looking at the vulva, looking to see the lips of the vagina open and the head of the child emerge. I can count on the fingers of one hand the number of women who have gotten up on the examining table and been fully present in their bodies. There are women who cover their vulvas, who make the obligatory remark about how they smell bad. I know that all of those feelings of shame and dirtiness have not always been there for us. The female vulva was once an emblem of beauty and holiness and transcendence. All humans come into the world through the gateway of our body.

"I'm a warrior for the body; I work with poor women, women who aren't claiming spirituality or even asking that their births be spiritual. One of the things that I do is to remind them that they can always say no. If you don't want to have sex, you have the right to say no. I encourage women to say yes and no in their relationships, and I tell them that their sexuality will exist throughout their lives and they need to think about caring for their body more. Sexuality has been important for me because it's been my entry into the realm of the spiritual, so that working with the vulva dance and working with the body is my service to the Goddess."[12]

This Is My Body

We produce symbols unconsciously and spontaneously in the form of dreams. Many women and men today are dreaming about the Goddess; she is a projection of the feminine principle that needs restoration in our culture. She takes many forms, often embodied in the rich symbols of a person's heritage. Catherine is a woman in her late forties who was raised in a strict Irish Catholic family. She recently had a series of dreams about the chalice, which in the Catholic mass is used in the transformation of wine into the blood of Christ. In pre-Christian cultures the chalice, or vessel, was a symbol of the feminine aspect of the sacred.

In the first dream she saw herself in a painting with the following inscription underneath: "This is She who drinks the chalice of the Holy Blood." One month later she had a dream in which she was drinking from the chalice and twelve drops of blood slid down her throat. She heard the words: "You are nurtured by the blood of the Great Mother." "Blood is a life-giving image," she wrote in her journal, "an image of renewal and regeneration. It is a powerful image of the feminine, that of vessel, that of womb, that of the cleansing and purification of menstrual blood. Drinking the blood of the Goddess is my sacred initiation into the mysteries of the feminine."

Two months later Catherine had a dream in which she saw her body as the chalice, and she heard the words: "This is my beloved daughter in whom I am well pleased." She awoke ablaze. "I was vibrating with energy," she wrote. "I couldn't stay in bed; I felt that my body would blow apart, I was so full. It was the middle of the night but I pulled out all of my art supplies and first fashioned a rudimentary chalice in clay. The temperature of the cool clay calmed me down some, but it wasn't enough. I needed color to represent how I felt. I took out all of my markers and drew a chalice alive with energy and vibrant with color. The words "this is my body, this is my blood" kept repeating in my mind. I realized at that moment that *I* embodied spirit; *my* body and *my* blood. I was the Goddess embodied, not in an arrogant way, but simply as the embodiment of spirit. God or Goddess is not separate from me, outside of myself; I embody Her, I feel Her power."

A Cap on My Heart

One does not make the descent lightly; it stirs up dust. To avoid feeling sad and helpless we have filled our lives as much as possible with important busyness, lest we become overwhelmed with unsafe emotions lurking in the depths. A woman who has the courage to descend into the realms below the surface of her ordinary awareness will find feelings there that she has chosen not to experience before. As she peels off the well-worn mask she presents to the collective fathers—being nice, polite, compliant, agreeable: "Oh, I don't care, anything you want to do"—she may find daggers of rage about time sacrificed, confusion about betrayals left unaddressed, sadness for having abandoned herself for so long, and help-lessness about taking the next step.

An attractive woman in her fifties who has raised ten children smiles and says, "I've been very happy all these years. I only regret the conversations I never had—with my children, with my husband, with myself. I put a cap on my heart because there was too much to do, there were too many disappointments, and I felt safe where I was and didn't want to rock the boat."

Too much to do. How many women have given themselves away because there was too much to do and no time to listen. Women who define themselves in relationship to their parents, spouses, siblings, children, or work associates have little en-ergy left over to consider *their* true feelings. Anyway, they have been told that thinking about themselves is selfish. Or their inflated self-importance prevents them from seeing their col-lusion in their codependence on others: "If *I* don't do it, it won't get done."

For centuries women have been told not to be "hysterical." If they felt strongly about something, they were not lauded for their commitment and passion but told that they were being unreasonable. If they expressed a grievance with anger they were told they were out of control.

Parents who are uncomfortable with the expression of feel-ings tell their daughters "Don't feel that way," or they taunt "Here comes Sarah Bernhardt" or "Get out the crying towel." In such families, joy can be expressed only in moderation as well; expressing too much happiness is considered being "too silly." When a child is repeatedly told that she is "too much" she learns that her feelings are not safe. She quickly realizes that sadness, disappointment, anger, or even excitement are not acceptable to parents and teachers, so why bother feeling at all. Feelings that are not acknowledged do not go away; they go underground and bind us to the past.

We cut ourselves off from our feelings because we do not want to experience the sadness of not being held and cherished like the worm baby in my dream. We do not want to hear the fury of her cry, the unspoken demand of our little girl within saying "How could you abandon me?" James Hillman calls it the *incestuous return to the mother.* This incestuous reunion with the mother involves "allowing oneself to join with the darkest bloodiest passions, the actual longings to be held and carried and caressed, the uninhibited rages and furies. It means going where the heart really is, where we actually feel, even if in the fists, guts, and genitals, rather than where the heart should be and how we ought to feel."[13] We might ache with this particular sadness with our whole bodies.

Grieving the Separation from the Feminine

One of the greatest challenges of the heroine's journey is to experience the deep sadness a woman feels about her separation from the feminine, to allow herself to name and grieve this loss in whatever way is appropriate for her, and to then release it and move on. When she is in a state of sadness and despair she needs the support of the positive feminine, a mother or sister figure, man or woman, to contain her safely while she expresses it. The intensity of the sadness varies with the degree to which a woman feels unseen and unknown to herself, and with how much she has to do to reclaim her lost treasures. She may feel sad for the simple reason of having too much and not having enough: having an abundance of "things" or empty accolades, but lacking self-love, self-respect, or connection to her inner core. It is important not to merely focus blame on others for this sorrow, but to deeply examine its causes and take responsibility for self-healing.

Angela is an incest survivor in her mid-twenties who has told her mother of her deep disappointment and anger at the mother's inability to protect her from her stepfather's molestation. Time and time again her mother told her that she had not known what was going on and refused to take the blame. She wouldn't listen to her daughter's feelings of helplessness and grief. Ten years of bitterness passed between the two women, until one day the mother came to the daughter and said, "I was wrong. I feel so terrible about not protecting you. I didn't want to see what was going on because I didn't know what to do about it. You have to know that I did the best I could at the time, but it just wasn't enough. I failed you." The daughter felt *heard* for the first time in her relationship with her mother. It did not eradicate the pain and humiliation of the incest, but in expressing her feelings and being heard she began to heal the wound. And out of her sadness she developed compassion for her mother.

"Sadness lies at the very core of being. Lay the heart bare of every other feeling and inevitably you will come upon sadness, ready, like the quickened seed, to put forth its green leaf."[14] One does not have to hold onto sadness, however. Releasing sadness is a discipline, like mindful breathing. Breathe in, you feel it, breathe out, you release it. Breathe in, a tear rolls down your cheek; breathe out, you feel gratitude for its warmth. Breathe in, and smile.[15] Be kind to yourself, take baby steps.

Grandmother Spider

When a woman returns from the underworld dragging her bag of bones behind her, she yearns to be comforted, held, and nurtured. There is a desire to crawl into the lap of a mother figure, to be held to her breast, soothed, and told "Everything is going to be okay." The Tewa Pueblo Indian people tell us of the "usual journey upward from the deepest dark underground, with Mole as the digger. When the people emerge they are blinded by the light and want to go back. Then a small feminine voice speaks to them, telling them to be patient and to uncover their eyes only very slowly. When at last they open their eyes they see the bent little old Spider Woman, grandmother of the Earth and of all life. She warns them about the temptations to quarrel and to have weapons and the sorrow that can come from them. She also tells them of corn and how to plant and tend it."[16]

We yearn for this quality of the feminine that is compassionate and instructive, that tells us how to take care of ourselves and warns us about getting caught up in petty fights and the desire to dominate. Spider Woman is concerned about the people; she is a preserver of life, a weaver of webs, a mentor and helper to those who struggle on the journey. She understands patience: how to not move into the light prematurely, holding the tension and letting things unfold in the appropriate time. She knows how to plant and nurture new seeds. These qualities of the feminine within a woman or a man help them find their true humanity.

In the Hopi creation myth, Grandmother Spider plays a central role in helping the people discover the meaning of life:

> After the Sun Spirit had created the First (lower) World and put living creatures in it, He was not satisfied with what had been done, feeling that the creatures did not understand life's meaning. He called Grandmother Spider and asked Her to go to the creatures and get them ready to move on. She did so.
>
> She led them on their ascent to the next world above. They improved for awhile, but then again Grandmother Spider was sent as the one to tell them and to lead them to the next higher world. Here they made villages and planted and lived together in peace. But the light was dim, the air cold. Grandmother Spider taught them how to weave and how to make pots, and for a long time they got on quite well.
>
> Then dissension began. And Grandmother Spider came and said they had to make some choices, and those who wished to change had to go further up. When with great difficulty they managed to get just below the "doorway in the sky," no one could see any way to get up there and through it.
>
> At that moment Grandmother Spider and Her young warrior god grandsons appeared. Seeds were planted to

grow high. Grandmother Spider urged the people to sing
without stopping. This helped the bamboo sprout finally
to reach up and through the "doorway in the sky."
Grandmother Spider told the people that they must
gather themselves and their belongings together, must
ponder deeply what needed to be changed before they
reached that doorway, and said She would return. "In the
Upper World," She said, "you must learn to be true
humans."[17]

Grandmother Spider and her grandsons entered the Upper
World first. While the people settled this new world she
watched over them. She stayed nearby, available to teach them
how to make whatever they needed, and she showed them
rituals to bring light and warmth into the world.

When all had been accomplished Grandmother Spider put
a lake over the hole through which they had come and told
the people how to prepare for their journeys and what to
anticipate. She reminded them of their origins and told them
to keep their sacred rituals, saying, "Only those who forget
why they came to this world will lose their way."[18]

We, like the first people, need feminine introspection and
wisdom to be whole human beings. Grandmother Spider helps
us to re-remember who we are and what our responsibility is
as stewards of this planet. She gives us teachings, songs, and
rituals to remind us to honor our connection to the cycles of
nature. If we feel deeply our interconnection with all species,
we will not dominate or destroy others.

Several years ago I interviewed Colleen Kelley, a ritualist
and artist from New Mexico, for a project I was photographing
entitled "Changing Woman: Contemporary Faces of the Goddess." She told me of a waking dream image of an old woman
who reminded me of Grandmother Spider. "While on pilgrimage to a sacred place in Arizona I had a visionary experience
of a very old woman who came out of the canyon toward me
and showed me many things. One of these things was a spirit
web that was breaking apart. This web was made of offerings
and ceremonies that have been done for thousands of years.
The message she brought was that to maintain this web of life

women who have been trying to keep these traditions alive are now reaching out in a telepathic way to women and men all over the world who are in tune with ceremony. Life will be threatened if the web is not maintained."[19]

The Feminine as Preserver

The preserver of life is one aspect of the positive feminine, whether embodied in a woman or a man. The positive feminine is concerned with networking and affiliation, with bringing communities together to work for the common good. The feminine sees similarities between all beings and exhibits compassion and mercy. It also demands protection for the young and less fortunate.

Käthe Kollwitz, a German artist, portrayed the exploited and unprotected worker, the joys and sorrows of motherhood, and the horrors of war in a way that embodied the preserver aspect of the feminine. In her posters "Germany's Children Are Hungry!," "Never Again War," and "Seed for the Planting Shall Not Be Ground Up," she protested the senseless destruction of human lives during World Wars I and II. Her sculpture "Tower of Mothers" shows the fierce, defiant protection of the feminine against forces that threaten the young. After her son was killed in the first World War, she expressed the mourning of an entire people in "The Parents."

During the distress and horror of Nazi Germany Kollwitz encouraged herself and others not to lose faith by drawing tender pictures of mothers and children to remind all of the warmth of human relationships.[20] She felt that her work had a purpose "to be effective in this time when people are so helpless and in need of aid."[21] In France, Romain Rolland called the work of Kollwitz the "greatest German poem" of her period. He wrote, "This woman of manly heart has looked on [the poor], has taken them into her motherly arms with a solemn and tender compassion. She is the voice for the silence of those who have been sacrificed."[22] Like the aspect of the feminine embodied in Kwan Yin, Kollwitz heard the cries of the people.

The Feminine as Creator:
Oshun and Changing Woman

A woman who has made the descent has experienced the devouring, destroyer aspect of the feminine, who is in the service of the death and renewal of herself. After the dryness and aridity experienced during this separation from life "above" she yearns for the moist, green, juicy aspect of the creative feminine. A woman who has felt cut off from her feminine nature may slowly begin to reclaim who she is as she feels creativity start flowing. This renewal may occur in the garden, in the kitchen, in decorating the home, in relationship, in weaving, writing, or dance. Her sense of aesthetics and sensuality come alive as she is refreshed by color, smell, taste, touch, and sound.

Oshun, the West African goddess of love, art, and sensuality, teaches us about beauty and creativity. Luisah Teish, a priestess of Oshun in the African tradition of Yoruba Lucumi, describes her as "the place where the river waters meet the ocean. She is not only the erotic love between couples but the love that gave the original impulse for creation. She is in every calla lily, every waterfall, and in the eyes of every child. Because of her we can exist in the world without fear; she makes life more than bearable. She embodies everything that is beautiful, that inspires people to have great imaginations to create exquisite works of art and to really use their senses. When I go into trance and create something that opens other people up, I know that she's there. Anytime I'm near a river where there are beautiful stones, I can hear her as clear as day."[23]

In Navaho mythology, Changing Woman is the creatrix. She is the earth and sky, the Lady of Plants and of the Sea. She goes beyond the bearer aspect of the mother; she is the feminine creator. She made the first human beings from skin rubbed from various parts of her body. She is forever changing and evolving. "Her cosmic cyclic movements—aging each winter and becoming a beautiful young maiden each spring— make Her the essence of death and rebirth, signature of the

continual restoration and rejuvenation of Life."[24] It is said that
"where masculine creativity tends to move always forward,
feminine creativity tends to turn round on itself, not circularly
so much as spirally."[25] It is constantly changing. Through
dance Changing Woman creates. This woman of incredible
beauty creates beauty wherever she goes. She wears a dress of
white shells and turquoise and dances a puberty ritual for all
young Navaho girls. This dance is described in the "Song of
the First Puberty Ceremony":

> She moves, she moves.
> She moves, she moves.
>
> White-Shell-Woman, she moves
> Her shoes of white shell, she moves
> Her shoes trimmed in black, she moves
> Her shoe-strings of white shell, she moves
> Her leggings of white shell, she moves. . . .
>
> Her dancing-skirt of white shell, she moves
> Her belt of white shell, she moves
> Her skirt of white shell, she moves
> Her bracelet of white shell, she moves
> Her necklace of white shell, she moves
> Her earrings of white shell, she moves. . . .
>
> Above her a male blue-bird dances about beautifully,
> she moves
> He sings: his voice is beautiful, she moves. . . .
>
> Before her all is beautiful, she moves
> Behind her all is beautiful, she moves.
>
> She moves, she moves
> She moves, she moves. [26]

This ability to move *with* the creative impulse without trying
to force it is an aspect of the feminine that I am only now
beginning to learn. Daughters of the father, like myself, have
a difficult time *allowing* things to happen; we like to control
events and their timing. Waiting for an outcome and the
uncertainty of the result create enormous anxiety. There is a
quality of the feminine that allows things to happen in the
natural cycle of things. People who work at deep levels of the

unconscious in therapy and in the creative process know that there are phases of both quietude and renewal, and these must be respected, protected, and given time. One cannot force birth. Trusting the mystery of manifestation is one of the deep teachings of the feminine journey.

Refining the Vessel

Finding out about *being* instead of *doing* is the sacred task of the feminine. In dreams and artwork, many women today are reclaiming the image of the vessel, which speaks to the inner-directed aspect of the feminine. The *vesica piscis* ("vessel of the fish") is a symbol of the feminine as vessel in both pagan and Christian religions. Joan Sutherland talks about refining the vessel, which is our life. "Meditation and that kind of solitary work refine the vessel from the inside, and communal ritual, joining together, and celebrating with other women refine it from the outside. We have to keep working on that vessel because the quality of that vessel determines what can happen in it, the nature of the transformation that can occur. We have to pay attention to that process of refinement so that the vessel can accept what is given to it, what comes through it. The refinement is both inside and outside until it becomes a transparent vessel, until the walls meet. And it's simple; it's not complicated. But it's hard, and it requires a real commitment to it."[27]

Being requires accepting oneself, staying within oneself and not *doing* to prove oneself. It is a discipline that is accorded no applause from the outside world; it questions production for production's sake. Politically and economically it has little value, but its simple message has wisdom: If I can accept myself as I am, and if I am in harmony with my surroundings, I have no need to produce, promote, or pollute to be happy. And being is not passive; it takes focused awareness.

Valerie Bechtol, an artist from New Mexico, creates spirit vessels that speak to this active aspect of being. "The spirit vessels that I create are a connection to myself as vessel, going in and realizing that everything I need is within me. I am an incredible vessel, a big, wonderful gigantic womb that is totally self contained. It doesn't matter where I am. I have a home in that vessel. Through my work, I want to break away from the passivity we place in this culture today on vessels. I want to reclaim the meaning from pagan times when the vessel was a very active instrument. It was transformational; the vessel was used to heal and it was always made by women."[28]

Perhaps that is because women understand what it is to be a vessel. They understand what it is to allow transformation to occur within their womb. If given support and respect to *be* who they are, women give birth to wisdom. And our planet, Gaia, needs this wisdom of mindful *being* to get into a right relationship with all living species. Our mindless *doing* has created incredible destruction on this earth.

That is why it is so necessary to redefine *hero* and *heroine* in our lives today. The heroic quest is not about power over, about conquest and domination; it is a quest to bring balance into our lives through the marriage of both feminine and masculine aspects of our nature. The modern-day heroine has to confront her fear about reclaiming her feminine nature; her personal power; her ability to feel, heal, create, change social structures, and shape her future. She brings us wisdom about the interconnectedness of all species; she teaches us how to live together in this global vessel and helps us to reclaim the feminine in our lives. We yearn for her:

> Oh, Great Grand-Mother,
> I have been a father's daughter,
> At last I am my mother's daughter.
>> Oh, Mother, forgive me, for I knew not what I did.
>> Oh, Mother, forgive me, even as I forgive you.
> Oh, Grand-Mother; oh, Great Grand-Mother,
>> We are coming home.
> We are woman.
> We are coming home.
>
> Nancee Redmond[29]

8

Healing the Mother/Daughter Split

The reality of our time in history requires that we
reverse the pattern of the fairytales—we must go back,
restore and heal these female constellations in order
to renew and integrate the suppressed masculine element.
Madonna Kolbenschlag, *Kiss Sleeping Beauty Goodbye*

It runs deep
this quest to unwind the shroud
that would bind the wound
that would mark us with blood
at the hye-tide of the red anemone
this first Sunday after
the first full moon of Spring,
that would call us back
to the origin of things
and would have us see
in the turning point of time
a reflection of the moon
in the redemption
of Love.
Julia Connor, "On the Moon of
the Hare"

The next stage of the heroine's journey involves healing what
I call the *mother/daughter split*, the split from one's feminine
nature. And for me this is the most difficult part of the journey
to write about, because it is the most painful aspect for me.
Like many women, I have discovered the powerful father
within and have developed the heroic qualities that society has
defined as male. I have developed those skills of discrimina-

Mother and Daughter. Painting by Meinrad Craighead.

tion, logical thinking, and follow-through that serve me well in the outer world. Several times in my life I have made the descent and have survived being scraped raw by Ereshkigal. Each time I have returned from the underworld with more of myself intact.

But I have not healed the mother/daughter split within myself. My relationship with my own mother has never been easy, but I feel that this wound goes beyond a woman's relationship with her personal mother. It goes to the heart of the imbalance in values within our culture. We have separated from our feelings and our spiritual natures. We are lonely for deep connection. We yearn for affiliation and community; for the positive, strong nurturing qualities of the feminine that have been missing from this culture. "When an individual or a society becomes too one-sided, too separated from the depth and truth of human experience, something in the psyche rises up and moves to restore authenticity. Breakdown momentarily sets life free from demands of ordinary reality and activates a profoundly spiritual process, an inner rite of passage with its own healing end."[1] We yearn for a strong, powerful female parent.

Daughters Unmothered

I, like many women, have never felt deeply mothered; although I know what it feels like to be deeply loved. My mother had a hard time accepting me; I was too much for her as a child. I was always falling out of trees, breaking limbs, or getting into accidents. She did not value my creative impulses; those impulses threatened her. She tried to contain me but I could not be contained. I kept breaking out of the vessel of her mothering. It was too small for me; it suffocated me.

In my early years I identified the feminine as smothering and dangerous. Although I recognized the beauty and sensuality of the feminine, to me it lacked humor. It sought perfection, and I certainly was less than a perfect child; my feelings didn't fit. I know that my initial rejection of the feminine was a rejection of my mother's anger, disapproval, rigidity, and inability to hear or see me as I was. As a young adolescent, the more I rejected her and identified with my father, the more I separated from the strong powerful feminine within myself.

Luckily, my mother was very involved with her religious life, and she encouraged my devotion to the spiritual. In fact, she was proud of the fact that I walked every day to early mass. I certainly didn't share with her the visions I had of St. Francis and the Virgin Mary, but I could spend hours creating altars and talking to saints, and she would leave me alone. When I was not at home I spent my time in the woods, near the brook with my favorite tree. I felt at home there, safe and protected.

My mother was happy to allow me all the time I needed to be alone because we rubbed each other the wrong way when we were together. She called me a know-it-all and told me that one day I would get myself into trouble. Of course she was right. With some frequency I created a stir with the nuns at school—especially when I questioned something that didn't make sense to me, like Christ's Resurrection. "How did Jesus get out of the tomb, Sister?" I asked in second grade. "He had already been dead for three days, and there was a large stone covering the opening."

Asking that question gained me immediate expulsion from class and entrance to the principal's office. From there I was sent home, where my mother was angry that I had offended the sisters. Another time in first grade the nun cracked a yardstick over my arm which caused such a welt that she was afraid to send me home. She needn't have feared. When I got home, I was punished for causing the nun to lose her temper.

Adolescence was a nightmare. When I fell in love with my first boyfriend at seventeen, my mother decided that I was possessed by the devil and set up an appointment with the local priest to exorcise me. Luckily he cancelled. She kept warning me that I'd better not come home pregnant but I was so sheltered that I didn't even know how that was accomplished! My mother had not initiated me into the mysteries of womanhood. By age twenty-one I had figured it out, and I actualized her worst fears by arriving home pregnant and engaged. She carried on unforgivably and called me a prostitute. My pregnant body, which I was so proud of, was scorned and ridiculed.

That is water under the bridge, turbulent at one time but becalmed now. In examining how this split from the feminine has affected my life I am aware that I have overridden my body, ignored its needs, and pushed it beyond exhaustion to illness. I have taken for granted the skills that come to me easily; I have ignored my intuition. I have felt guilty about taking time to relax or to incubate. I have expected struggle instead of ease and have not fully enjoyed this precious gift of life. I hear similar stories from other women who in their childhood were told to work hard, produce, please, and ignore their feelings. There was no expectation of ease in life, and *enjoying* life was unheard of. Instead they were told: "Life is hard, life is not fair; if you want to relax, wait until you're pushing up the daisies."

In working through much of the anger that was left unexpressed during my childhood and adolescence, I have found deep healing in the art of mothering. Being a parent and then a teacher has taught me how to nurture, empower, and play with others. Like many women who experienced a lack of mothering in their childhood, I have found my deepest healing in the active mothering role. In my early thirties I searched for Mother in the love and approval of older women who were my mentors or work associates. In my late thirties I remarried after finding a man who is very comfortable with his own feminine nature. I have been deeply nurtured by his love.

I cherish my relationship with my sister and women friends and have for years been involved in women's groups and rituals to honor female rites of passage. But I still carry an urgent yearning to connect with Mother. Part of it comes from the knowledge that there are conversations I will never have with my own mother, and part of it comes from a desire to be whole.

I know that the mother/daughter split affects my relationship to the inner feminine. I also know that until I can heal that wound I will not be complete. I feel the helplessness of a newborn separated from her mother; to heal this inner split I have to develop a nurturing mother within myself.

Mother as Fate

Whether our personal mother was nurturing or cold, empowering or manipulative, present or absent, our internal relationship with her is integrated into our psyche as the *mother-complex*. James Hillman writes about how this complex is basic to our most permanent and intractable feelings about ourselves:

> One faces the mother, as fate, ever again and anew. Not only the contents of feelings, but the function itself takes patterns from the reactions and values which come to life in the mother-child relationship. The way we feel about our bodily life, our physical self-regard and confidence,

the subjective tone with which we take in or go out into the world, the basic fears and guilts, how we enter into love and behave in closeness and nearness, our psychological temperature of coldness and warmth, how we feel when we are ill, our manners, taste, and style of eating and living, habitual structures of relating, patterns of gesture and tone of voice, all bear the marks of mother.[2]

For a woman the mother-complex has enormous implications in regard to her self-identity and sexual feelings, and these may have nothing to do with how she perceived her mother's ease or discomfort with her own body. Hillman continues:

> These influences upon the feeling function do not have to be copied after the personal mother, nor even be contradictory to her in order for the mother-complex to show its effect. The mother-complex is not my mother; it is my complex. It is the way in which my psyche has taken up my mother.[3]

If a woman's psyche "has taken up" her mother in a negative or destructive way, she splits from her positive feminine nature and has much work to do to reclaim it. If her mother's attitudes threaten her very survival as a woman, she may identify closely with the masculine, seeking salvation in it. Many women have found the spontaneous, fun-loving, nurturing aspect of the feminine within their fathers.

The nature of the mother/daughter split is also determined by how a woman integrates the archetypal Mother into her psyche, which includes Mother Earth and the cultural view of the feminine.

Our collective psyche fears the power of Mother and does everything it can to denigrate and destroy it. We take her nurturance for granted; we use, abuse, and dominate matter (*mater*) every time we get the chance. Every barrel of oil that pours into Prince William Sound, every ton of nuclear waste that is stored in the New Mexican desert, every tree that is suffocated by acid rain shows our enormous arrogance and disregard for her.

Our churches have pushed the feminine face of God underground for centuries, destroying her image and usurping her
power for the male gods. How can we feel connected to the
feminine when the culture around us does everything in its
power to make us forget? We bow before the gods of greed,
domination, and ignorance and scoff at feminine images of
nurturance, balance, and generosity. We rape, plunder, and
destroy the earth and expect her to give to us endlessly. This
mother/daughter wound runs deep; it will take much to
heal it.

The Search for the Personal Mother

I wonder if the pain associated with the mother/daughter split
originates at birth, when the daughter is no longer fused with
the mother and longs for that safe, secure environment to
contain her once more. Somewhere in our psyche we all yearn
for the warmth of the amniotic fluid gently bathing and
rocking us to life. We miss the reassuring sound of her heart
pulsing within us. If the separation from the mother occurs
too soon or the connection with the mother is lost at birth, a
woman will search for her mother throughout her life.

Rose-Emily Rothenberg writes about the experience of a
child orphaned at birth:

> At a very early age, the mother represents the Self. A
> living connection to the mother who carries this impor-
> tant life-giving projection is crucial to the newborn's sense
> of security and self-worth. The mother also carries a
> connection that goes all the way back to the earth. When
> there has been damage to this fundamental primary
> relationship [the child's] ego is turned prematurely back
> into itself and reduced to its own resources. The infant
> then experiences abandonment. . . .[4]

Feeling abandoned by the mother is an issue for unorphaned
women as well. Whether the mother was physically present or
not, the lack of her emotional and spiritual presence is felt as
abandonment by the child. Incest survivors who were molested
by male relatives and adult children of alcoholics relate the

excruciating pain of being abandoned by mothers too over-whelmed or self-involved to be protective of and present for their children. Throughout their lives these children continue to ask others for attention, approval, and a definition of self in their urgent need to be mothered.

If a woman recognizes the wound of her inner feminine, and her mother is still alive and available, she may seek to heal that wound by renewing and transforming this initial relationship. She recognizes the fragmentation she carries from being an unmothered daughter and reaches out to ask for connection. In her article "How the Father's Daughter Found Her Mother," Jungian analyst Lynda Schmidt writes about finding a relationship in middle age with her mother, Jane Wheelwright.

Schmidt was mothered by nature, growing up with little supervision on a ranch just like her mother had before her. She grew up in the Artemis mode, without supervision except by the cowboys who were "good daddy" figures. "Because of their special vision and drive, my mother and father had business in the world that really could not include rearing children in the conventional way. For me, then, the major resource of my life was the wilderness, nature (which is the Great Mother/Female Self) in an unarticulated form. My principle mother was, therefore, an archetype, an atmosphere, a geography. There was minimal flesh and blood personal mothering. . . .[5]

She found that the "Great Mother-Ranch" was an excellent model for the female world, and it provided her with a strong connection to her instinctual and biological self, but she had little connection to her own mother until her middle years. At that time she read the original transcript of her mother's book, *The Death of a Woman,* which was basically a mother/daughter story about Wheelwright's relationship with a dying female cancer patient. For the first time Schmidt experienced her mother as *Mother.* Although the story was about her mother's relationship with another young woman, Schmidt was able to feel her capacity to be "motherly and concerned, even perhaps toward me. And this feeling opened up the second half of my life."[6]

Schmidt found common ground with her mother when they spent time together on the ranch, which had been mother to them both. There they developed an equality, a sisterly relationship. They found they could meet one another in their mutual love of horsepacking and in the world of ideas, working out the mother/daughter relationship in their writing and presentations. Now they share their healing with other women through workshops on mother/daughter relationships.

Women whose mothers have died or were unavailable for other reasons search for their mothers in dreams, in nature, and in their art. In "Persephone's Search for Her Mother" Patricia Fleming writes of her own yearning for Mother. Fleming was orphaned when her mother died twenty-eight hours after her birth in Uruguay. She was raised for the first five years of her life by her grandmother and was then painfully separated from her when her father remarried. She sought her mother in her relationship with her husband, daughter, friends, and associates, but it wasn't until the near death of her pregnant daughter and the loss of the unborn child that she was able to heal the feminine within. She grieved for her mother, her grandmother, for her daughter's pain, and for the unborn child:

> That spring when the iris were out, I found I wanted to paint iris, nothing but iris. Painting these deeply feminine shapes seemed to fill some need in me and to build a bridge to the deep feminine within myself. In the story of Demeter you will remember that Zeus finally takes pity on Demeter and her tears and sent Iris "on her wings of gold," according to Homer, as a gesture of reconciliation. In the myth it was the first golden bridge to the mother—to Demeter—to the earth—*to the ordinary*."[7]

Fleming continued her healing process through a pilgrimage to Greece, which seemed to her to be the land of the Mother. There she visited the sacred sites of the Goddess which honored Artemis, Isis, and Demeter. Her first experience of

Demeter was at the small museum at Tegea, where the carving of Demeter reminded her so much of her grandmother that she felt an immedite recognition of acceptance. At Eleusis she sat at the Sacred Well of Demeter and was deeply moved by the shock and trauma experienced by Demeter in her separation from Persephone. Fleming finally felt that her own suffering had some meaning, and she felt restored and redeemed by her kinship with Demeter.

After this experience a dream of her grandmother helped Fleming come to peace with her search for her mother. In the dream she asked her dead grandmother where she would like to be buried. Her grandmother said it was her choice, but if she decided to take her home she would always be with her. Fleming agreed to take her coffin home and put it in her living room. She realized in this dream that she had internalized the Mother/Grandmother. Her search for her mother was indeed over. [8]

Divine Ordinariness

Women who have experienced a deep wounding in relationship to their mothers often seek their healing in the experience of the ordinary. For many this takes the form of *divine ordinariness:* seeing the sacred in each ordinary act, whether it be washing the dishes, cleaning the toilet, or weeding the garden. Woman is nurtured and healed by grounding herself in the ordinary. Very often during this period of reclaiming the inner feminine, she identifies with Hestia and finds the Wise Woman Within.

"Hestia is the center of the Earth, the center of the home, and our own personal center. She does not leave her place; we must go to her."[9] She is the place of our inner wisdom. In ancient Greece Hestia was both the virginial goddess of the hearth and the hearth fire of a home. The hearth still represents the center of a home, a shelter from the elements, the place where family and friends gather in companionship. The values associated with Hestia are those of warmth, security, and human relationship. The Hestia in a family or an organization is the "spider" who weaves the webs, takes care of details, and knows what everyone is doing.

As women have taken more of a role in the outer world, the hearth of the family has been left unattended, and the spirit of nurturing connection has deteriorated. The value of the feminine as the center of the family has been largely ignored in society's devaluation of women. As home and hearth have lost significance, so too have we forgotten to value and protect our home planet. Women have had to leave the hearth to remind humankind of the importance of caring for their physical bodies as well as for the body of our collective household, the planet earth. [10]

Healing in Nature and Community

Many women today are focusing on the art of affiliation in a new way. In their desire to heal the split with their inner feminine, they are reaching out to other women, coming together to name their experience of the sacred, honoring their connection with Gaia, and undergoing female rites of passage through women's gatherings and vision quests. [11] Healing the mother/daughter split is a cocreated journey; to hear her own voice and to affirm her direction, a woman needs a supportive community.

In nature, woman is healed from her weary quest in the arms of Gaia, the original Mother. "She is more soil than mother and too huge, too distant to have the characteristics generally associated with a human mother." [12] All living matter is born from her. Her generous bosom reminds us of our fertility. She reflects to us our own cyclic nature: the times to hibernate and to give birth. The first flowers of spring, geese flying north, winds blowing through tall grasses, and salmon spawning remind us of the renewal of life. Winter solstice gives us permission to rest and gather our dreams.

Women once again are coming together to celebrate the seasons and to honor their connection with the phases of the moon. Mothers have begun to create rites of first menstruation with their pubescent daughters and to celebrate their own cessation of blood flow through rites of menopause. Through wilderness vision quests, women find the courage to overcome their personal fears while being supported by a community of women of all ages. They sing, dance, and fast together and listen alone in silence to the stories of sister snake, brother hawk, and sister moon. They pray for a vision of their true path. Women are sharing their dreams of a future that incorporates values of the heart, language that is inclusive, and images that celebrate life.

Grandmother as Guide

Many women call upon the image of Grandmother as a guide to the mysterious realms of the feminine. A woman's grandmother may be remembered as a safe haven, a source of nourishment, a caretaker during times of illness. Like Hecate, Grandmother Spider, and Hestia, she embodies qualities of feminine insight, wisdom, strength, and nurturance which may be missing from a woman's daily life. We call upon this crone aspect of the feminine to help us through difficult transitions.

While going through a time in her late twenties in which she was trying to understand the direction of her life's work, psychotherapist Flor Fernandez called upon the image of her grandmother, Patricia, in Cuba.

"My grandmother had always been a source of inspiration and strength for me. I grew up surrounded by her aura of protection and healing. I watched her heal others with her prayers, herbs, and rituals. I was a curious child, and she took the time to talk to me about her work as a *curandera* or healer. When I was five I became very ill with *mal de ojos*. (According to beliefs, this illness results from being looked at by a person who has negative energy or thoughts. The symptoms are vomiting and diarrhea, which I had at the time.)

"My grandmother took me into her healing room, lit candles, and proceeded to chant and pray. A few minutes later I was fine and ready to go out and play with my friends. My grandmother kept me in the room, however, and taught me a prayer for protection, calling upon a spiritual guide to help me in future occasions.

"I left my grandmother when I was fifteen to come to this country. For many years I forgot my connection to her and her healing work. I needed to assimilate a new culture where the work of my grandmother was considered superstitious. When I was twenty-eight I began to remember her again. I was going through a difficult time, what you might call an existential crisis. I had lost my roots and my soul, and I was feeling empty and lost.

"At that time I went to a workshop on death and dying and dreams, and there was a moment in the workshop when I looked at the woman leader and saw the face of my grandmother. I felt a current of energy going straight into my heart, lifting me up to a realm of knowing that I had forgotten. That night I dreamed about her. She came to me and said: 'Remember my child the times when I used to sit you in my lap and talk to you about healing herbs and how to collect them at the proper time so that the strength and power of the plant is preserved. We used to spend much time together talking about human nature and about forces unseen but felt. You were a different child, and I took the time to be with you because I knew you could carry on my teachings in the future. You have forgotten as I once did the mystery of our woman nature.' "[13]

This dream was the beginning of Fernandez's journey of becoming a healer. She started first with the healing of her own body and has continued to channel that energy into the healing of others. Many other women remember the particular gifts and talents of their grandmothers as they reclaim their own feminine nature.

Woman as Mythmaker

Mythmaking is an ongoing process, and myths are necessary to organize life. In discussing the definition of myth in the context of poetry Mark Schorer writes: "Myths are the instruments by which we continually struggle to make our experience intelligible to ourselves. A myth is a large, controlling image that gives philosophical meaning to the facts of ordinary life; that is, which has organizing value for experience. A mythology is a more or less articulated body of such images, a pantheon. Without such images, experience is chaotic, fragmentary and merely phenomenal. It is the chaos of experience that creates them, and they are intended to rectify it."[14]

If a woman has not been initiated into a feminine mythology by her mother or grandmother she has to develop her own relationship to her inner feminine, to the Great Mother. This may explain why so many women today seek ancient images of powerful feminine deities and heroines to heal the wound within. Because female history has been so shattered, women are reaching back to prehistory to find elements of the woman's mythology that existed before the Greek division of power into multiple gods. As archeologists uncover ancient cultures based on the life-giving principles of the Goddess, women reclaim the power and dignity once accorded to them, when the role of woman was to protect human life and the sacredness of nature.

Since the 1970s women artists have created an outpouring of images representing pre-Christian goddess figures and symbols associated with them. "Women artists such as Mary Beth Edelson, Carolee Schneemann, Mimi Lobell, Buffie Johnson, Judy Chicago, Donna Byars, Donna Henes, Miriam Sharon, Ana Mendieta, Betsy Damon, Betye Saar, Monica Sjoo, and Hannah Kay, by summoning up the powers associated with the Goddess archetype, are energising a new form of Goddess consciousness, which in its most recent manifestation is exorcising the patriarchal creation myth through a repossession of the female visionary faculties."[15]

The vision and power of the feminine is represented in depictions of the Virgin, Mother, and Crone; the spider, snake, and bird; the vessel, cave, and grail; the mountain, water, and trees; as well as specific cultural goddess figures such as Cerridwen, Lilith, Coatlicue, Kwan Yin, Yemaya, Tiamat, Amaterasu, and many, many more. These works capture the essence of the feminine aspects of creatrix, preserver, and destroyer and celebrate the preservation of, reverence for, and interconnection of the basic elements of life.[16]

In *Women as Mythmakers: Poetry and Visual Art by Twentieth-*

Century Women, Estella Lauter explains that myth usually takes the form of an unusually potent story or symbol that is repeated in the dreams of individuals or has its origins in group ritual. [17] She writes, "Once a myth is in place it is nearly impossible to dislodge it by exclusively rational means. It must be replaced by another equally persuasive story or symbol." [18]

Women are challenging prevailing myths about ancient symbols of the feminine—such as Eve, still used to distort women's power. In describing her paintings, Los Angeles artist Nancy Ann Jones says: "We have to challenge the tyranny of the biblical Eve depicted as a temptress with a profane and unclean body, held responsible by mankind for original sin for thousands of years. This myth has reinforced the stand that women should always have second-class citizenship because they were created after Adam from his rib. In all prohibitions placed on women, Eve is used as the validation." [19]

Jones continues by explaining the symbols in her work *Challenging Myth III* (see p. 47): "Here I have portrayed Eve in front of the maze inscribed on the floor of Chartres because Chartres was built on a site that was sacred to the goddess before Christianity existed. Centuries before the Old Testament was written, the goddess was worshipped and woman's sexuality was sacred. I want to see woman's sexuality restored to its original power and dignity. [20] Artists such as Jones who are creating new stories and symbols about the feminine are healing their own feminine nature in the process.

The Origin of Images of the Goddess

Early symbols of the Goddess probably had their origin in human reverence for female creativity in childbirth. Images of the mother became sacred. Mayumi Oda, an artist who was born during World War II in Japan and is now based in Sausalito, began painting the Goddess during the 1960s, during which time she was giving birth to her own children. She was concerned about giving birth to sons during the Vietnam War and was determined to find a positive female image with whom she could identify to give her the power to create and live. She had no previous conscious knowledge of the Goddess nor desire to paint goddess images; they merely came out of her.

"At that time I was doing etchings using black ink. Etching is quite a black medium. Out of this black seed, this huge woman with big breasts appeared. I titled her 'The Birth of Venus,' and that was definitely the birth of my own Goddess."[21]

She has continued to explore the different aspects of herself through goddess imagery for the past twenty years.

"When I didn't know my anger very well I tried to do peaceful goddesses. I did a painting of Kwan Yin as a compassionate goddess with a sword and titled it 'O Goddess Give Us Strength to Cut Through.' I realized that compassion is something that is not just sympathy but is more ruthless. For the past few years I have worked with the Black Dakini, which is the wrathful side of the female, the warrior side. Only through a practice of being gentle with myself could I do this. When I was angry I couldn't do it. It is not the anger that I wanted to express; it's beyond that. It's the dualism that we have to go beyond to meet our death."[22]

Many artists address the link between the Goddess and nature. Buffie Johnson, a New York artist in her late seventies, has been painting the Goddess in her nature forms since she was eight years old. "I was called to this work at a very young age, but I didn't know that at the time. When I was seven or eight I was living in the house of an old sea captain relative in Duxbury, Massachusetts with my aunt and grandmother, and I made forty illustrations of spirits of the sun, moon, stars, north wind, east wind, earth, and sky. All of them were women in different poses."[23]

In her thirties she began to collect images of the Great Mother. She became aware that she was painting the goddess of vegetation in her flower paintings. "One day I woke up and said, 'Well, I'm painting the goddess of vegetation because I have done the bud, the flower, the fruit, the pod and the root, the whole cycle of the Lady of Vegetation.'" She then researched the Goddess for thirty-five years and compiled her findings of the first known artifacts made by humankind to prove the existence of the Goddess in her book, *Lady of the Beasts*.

When I asked her why she painted the Goddess she replied, "The earth is in danger and we're in danger because we're part of the earth. Contrary to the Christian notion that plants, animals, minerals, and oceans are here to serve mankind, we are interconnected and we have to learn to be in oneness with the world instead of controlling it."[24]

The Dark Dream Woman

Women today are dreaming about strong, nurturing women who have no need to dominate others to exhibit power but who come to the dreamer to wake her up to a new order. They dream of the dark, of the need to face the harsh realities of life and death, of the possibility of cataclysm, suffering, and psychosis. Many dreamers encounter a large, powerful, dark-skinned woman who nurtures them and creates them anew.

Following kidney surgery a woman in her mid-forties had the following dream in which she experienced the descent, the meeting with the *dark dream woman*, and the healing of her feminine wound.

"I realize that I'm descending into hell. I put on my red parka. I want to return to the earth world.

"I'm surrounded by skeletons and ghouls. My skin is eaten off my body by gnashing teeth. I'm bones walking among bones. The wind begins to blow, and I become very dry. I'm on a desert, my bones dry and crumbling into a pile of dust. A drop of clear water drops into the little pile of bone dust that is me.

"A dark woman, an African or Indian woman, stirs the dust with her fingers to make a pasty mud. She begins to remake me. She starts with my vagina. My human body starts to cry. She's making me a woman first.

"As my body is completed I see that it is the same body that I'm in now. My scar from surgery is still there. My breasts still sag from nursing. Oh, it's this body that I get for this world.

I'm not dead yet. I'm alive in this body and in this world. A transformed body is for another place."

This was a powerful transformational dream which presaged enormous changes in this woman's perception of herself and her life. The dark dream woman may also come with a direct message for the dreamer.

I recently had a dream in which a thin black woman with no extra flesh to spare on her limbs sat in my kitchen rolling limes across the chopping block with her open palm. She wore a thread-bare housecoat. She looked at me, a bit tired but with life in her eyes, and said: "Girl, I have traveled the world over looking for my work and have come home to writing. Find your words, girl."

Woman's Words

As more and more people create images and stories of the sacred feminine, these become solidified in language and influence the experience of others. Susan Griffin has renamed the earth "sister" instead of mother, whore, or crone, and in so doing she has given us an accessible love for nature that is not separate from us.

In her poem "This Earth: What She Is to Me," Griffin identifies her grief, empathy, eros, and solace in her relationship with earth as sister. Her words bring deep healing.

> As I go into her, she pierces my heart. As I penetrate further, she unveils me. When I have reached her center, I am weeping openly. I have known her all my life, yet she reveals stories to me, and these stories are revelations and I am transformed. Each time I go to her I am born like this. Her renewal washes over me endlessly, her wounds caress me; I become aware of all that has come between us, of the noise between us, the blindness, of something sleeping between us. Now my body reaches out to her. They speak effortlessly, and I learn at no instant does she fail me in her presence. She is as delicate as I am; I know her sentience; I feel her pain and my own pain comes into me, and my own pain grows large and I grasp this pain with my hands, and I open my mouth to

this pain, I taste, I know, and I know why she goes on, under great weight, with this great thirst, in drought, in starvation, with intelligence in every act does she survive disaster. This earth is my sister; I love her daily grace, her silent daring, and how loved I am *how we admire this strength in each other, all that we have lost, all that we have suffered, all that we know: we are stunned by this beauty,* and I do not forget: what she is to me, what I am to her."[25]

Taking Back the Dark:
Reclaiming the Madwoman

I opened this chapter with Madonna Kolbenschlag's quote about restoring and healing female constellations in fairy tales because I feel it is imperative that we reclaim and reintegrate the repressed parts of the feminine which are embodied as witches, evil stepmothers, and madwomen. Fairy tales are usually told from the perspective of a young girl (or boy) and revolve around her relationship to parents, siblings, magical creatures, and people she meets along the path. We hear how she responds to good or evil treatment by others, how she meets the challenges throughout her journey, and how she finally achieves her boon of success or reconciliation.

Stepmothers, witches, and madwomen are characteristically portrayed as women who present obstacles to the developing child. They are described as mean, cruel, withholding, manipulative, jealous, and greedy. Their wicked deeds are usually punished by death. The witch is pushed into an oven in "Hansel and Gretel"; the stepmother in "Snow-White and the Seven Dwarfs" dances to her death in slippers that have been heated over hot coals; and the Wicked Witch of the West melts in the "Wizard of Oz."

In the fairy tale there is little concern for the origins of cruelty in the stepmother or wicked witch; we just assume that she was always that way. We never get to hear her side of the story about the whining, disobedient, manipulative child who is, of course, the apple of her father's eye. The wicked stepmother represents the disappointment each child carries at not having the "perfect" mother, that illusory mother-next-

door who is ever-present, ever-understanding, and uncondi-
tionally loving.

There is a folktale, however, in which the daughter opens
the door and takes back her mother, healing those repressed
parts of the feminine that we choose not to see and refuse to
accept and understand. This tale of a rejected daughter who
heals the outcast within herself by healing the madwoman
who is her mother was first told to me by storyteller Kathleen
Zundell. What follows is my adaptation of that tale.

Once upon a time there lived a woman with four daughters.
She loved her daughters One, Two, and Three who were
clever, fair, and beautiful, but hated her youngest, who was
just who she was. Each day she went out to gather food for
her children. As she returned, her daughters would hear her
sing:

> My darling daughters,
> One, two, and three,
> Come to Mama, come to me.
> Mesmeranda, daughter four,
> Stay behind the kitchen door.

The girls ran to the door to let their mother in, but
Mesmeranda stayed behind the kitchen door. Then the mother
prepared dinner for the three older daughters and as they ate
together, talking and laughing, they threw the leftovers to
Mesmeranda. The older girls grew and prospered and Mesmeranda remained thin and frail.

Now there lurked outside a wolf who watched the mother's
comings and goings and hungered for her three plump daughters. He thought he could catch them by singing the mother's
song. He practiced for days and nights and one afternoon
while she was away, he went to the door and sang:

> My darling daughters,
> One, two, and three,
> Come to Mama, come to me.
> Mesmeranda, daughter four,
> Stay behind the kitchen door.

Nothing happened. The girls did not open the door because
the voice of the wolf was low and gruff. Foiled, the wolf went

off to see Coyote. "I need a mother's voice," he said. "Make my voice sound high and sweet." Coyote looked at the wolf. "What will you give me in return?" he asked. "One of the mother's daughters," replied the wolf. Coyote tuned the wolf's voice and the wolf returned to the house of the daughters and sang:

> My darling daughters,
> One, two, and three,
> Come to Mama, come to me.
> Mesmeranda, daughter four,
> Stay behind the kitchen door.

This time the wolf's voice was so high it flew on the wind. The girls laughed and said to each other, "Oh, that's just the leaves whispering," and did not open the door. Some time later the mother returned and sang her song to her daughters. At once they opened the door and again the four ate, leaving the leftovers for Mesmeranda.

The next day the wolf returned to Coyote and complained. "You made my voice too thin. Fix it so I sound like a woman." Coyote cast a spell on the wolf and the wolf returned to the house of the daughters. This time he sang just like the mother:

> My darling daughters,
> One, two, and three,
> Come to Mama, come to me.
> Mesmeranda, daughter four,
> Stay behind the kitchen door.

The girls ran to greet their mother, and the wolf stuffed them into a sack and carried them off. Mesmeranda remained behind the kitchen door.

Later that day the mother returned and sang at the door:

> My darling daughters,
> One, two, and three,
> Come to Mama, come to me.
> Mesmeranda, daughter four,
> Stay behind the kitchen door.

No one came to the door, so she sang her song again. Again no one came, and she began to fear the worst. Then she heard a faint voice singing:

> Mama, your daughters,
> One, two, and three,
> Can no longer hear, can no longer see.
> They've gone away, beyond land and sea.
> Mesmeranda is here, look at me.

The mother threw open the door and when she did not see her beloved daughters, she ran from the house like a madwoman, pulling at her hair and singing her song over and over.

Mesmeranda stood up, saw the empty room, and walked out the open door. She began her journey, made her way in the world, and eventually married the emperor's son.

Time passed. One day an old madwoman, whose hair was wild and tangled like a hornet's nest, was heard singing at the palace gate:

> My darling daughters,
> One, two, and three,
> Can no longer hear, can no longer see.
> Mesmeranda, daughter four,
> Hear me now, I'm at your door.

People laughed as they passed her by and the palace guards told her to move on. But each day she returned in her tattered rags and sang:

> My darling daughters,
> One, two, and three,
> Can no longer hear, can no longer see.
> Mesmeranda, daughter four,
> Hear me now, I'm at your door.

Word reached the empress that there was a madwoman in the streets singing for her daughter Mesmeranda. Mesmeranda said, "I know no madwoman and I have no mother."

One day Mesmeranda was planting flowers in the palace garden and heard her name in the madwoman's refrain. She opened the gate and looked into the face of the madwoman. There she saw her mother. She took her hand and brought her in.

"Mama," she said, "the others are gone. But look at me. I am Mesmeranda. You did not love me before and I stayed behind the kitchen door. But now I am here and I will take care of you." Then she bathed her mother, dressed her, and brushed out her hair.

Reclaiming the Power of the Feminine

Mesmeranda takes her mother back, cleanses her, clothes her, and cares for her. She opens up her heart and takes back the Madwoman who was the mother who rejected her. Each one of us has to take back the discarded feminine in order to reclaim our full feminine power. If a woman continues to resent her mother for the lack of mothering she received, she remains bound to this woman, a perennial daughter-in-waiting. She refuses to grow up, although to the outside world she appears to function as a mature adult. In her depths, she feels unworthy and incomplete. In *The Pregnant Virgin* Marion Woodman names this outcast part of ourselves "the pregnant virgin": "the part who comes to consciousness through going into darkness, mining our leaden darkness, until we bring her silver out."[26]

Many women are unaware of how they hold themselves back in life because of messages they received from their "mothers" (mother, grandmother, aunts, and family friends) in childhood. These litanies served to immobilize their mothers and continue to shackle the spirit of their daughters: "I should have been . . ." "I always wanted to be . . ." "You don't know how painful it is not to have anything for myself." . . . "I never had time for myself." . . . "Your father wouldn't let me. . . ." "Don't get into trouble." . . . "Don't hurt anyone's feelings." . . . "I can't take it . . ." "I'm overwhelmed . . ." "I'm going to go crazy . . ." "I don't know how other people do it . . ." "I can't stand this pain."

"I can't stand this pain" was a direct command not to feel. One German-American mother told her daughter not to tell the neighbors how she felt about anything: "We don't do that in this family." If the daughter told her mother she was upset about what had happened with her friends at school, her mother told her not to feel that way. Taking back the dark for this daughter means moving beyond shame to reclaim *all* of the feelings she hid from herself, no matter how frightening, so that she can find her authentic voice.

A client in her late forties grew up with a mother who was hard of hearing. Her role in that relationship was to protect her mother, interpret for her, and speak for her. She had no presence of her own other than to be her mother's go-between. "I learned how to be invisible at an early age. I also learned what other people wanted. I never had the opportunity to express what I wanted because there was no one there to hear me or to affirm my wishes. I quit wanting. I became invisible to myself. It is only now, as I approach fifty, that I am learning how important it is for me to be visible outside as well as inside, to be acknowledged and praised for what I know, and to ask for what I want."

Daughters who did not have mothers who could back them up in their childhood felt that they had to know how to do everything for themselves. This is a typical attitude of adult children of alcoholics. They have difficulty as adults asking for help and seeking out what they need because this type of guidance was never available. In adulthood they continue to do things themselves, fearing that they can never rely on anyone else. They feel that they must perform perfectly to hide what they don't know and were never taught. Learning to ask for help is a big step in taking back their personal power.

I find it difficult to accept and cherish the madwoman within my mother because then I will have to face the madwoman within myself. If I take back my mother the way she is, I have to come to terms with the fact that I can't make her love me the way I want to be loved. I will never have a mommy who openly loves: a mother, yes, but not a mommy. I have to accept my mother as she is. I cannot hold onto the pain of a daughter unmothered; it prevents me from being all that I am.

During an imagery exercise of contacting my inner ally, the eagle comes to me, and I ask her what holds me back. She answers:

"Your resentment holds you back. Stop being resentful about lack, about what you didn't receive from your mother. It gives you excuses. Forgive your mother. Use the vision of an eagle to see beyond your personal loss or else your feelings will become distorted. Don't be a mouse, stuck looking at the end of your nose."

9

Finding the Inner Man with Heart

Your inner man and inner woman
have been at war
they are both wounded
tired
and in need of care
it is time
to put down the sword
that divides them in two

Healing the Wounded Masculine

In the legend of the Holy Grail, Parsifal searched for the Grail, the chalice used by Christ at the Last Supper and the ancient cauldron of the Great Goddess. Parsifal ventured into the Grail Castle, where he saw the Fisher King with a wound in his genitals or thigh, a wound that would not heal. The Grail itself could heal him, he needed a young innocent such as Parsifal to see that something was wrong, to have compassion, and to ask "What ails thee?" Only then would the healing qualities of the Grail become available to the king.

The King is the ruling principle in our psyches and in our culture, and we are like the Fisher King in our wounding. We are also like Parsifal, a "perfect fool" in our innocence. We are blind to the fact that we are out of balance. Until an aspect of ourselves recognizes our pain, has compassion, and asks "What ails thee?" we will not be healed.

We are split off from a relationship with our creative feminine; our rational mind devalues and ignores it as we refuse to listen to our intuition, feelings, the deep knowings of our

body. "As we have moved more and more into the realm of
logos over eros, left brain over right, there has been an
increasing sense of alienation from that inarticulate source of
meaning that can be called the feminine, the Goddess, the
Grail."[1] We feel the sadness and the loneliness of alienation,
but we do not recognize that these feelings result from an
imbalance within our nature.

The masculine is an archetypal force; it is not a gender.
Like the feminine, it is a creative force that lives within all
women and men. When it becomes unbalanced and *unrelated to
life* it becomes combative, critical, and destructive. This unrelated archetypal masculine can be cold and inhuman; it does
not take into account our human limitations. Its machismo
tells us to forge ahead no matter what the cost. It demands
perfection, control, and domination; nothing is ever enough.
Our masculine nature, like the Fisher King, is wounded.

The Grail is the symbol of the sacred, creative feminine
principle which is accessible to all of us. The Grail can heal
the King just as the feminine can heal our masculine nature.
In the legend, the Grail was carried at all times by the Grail
Maiden, but Parsifal and the king did not see it. "The Grail,
its castle and its guardians are bewitched owing to an act of
disrespect represented as an insult, rape, assault of its maidens,
disrespect of the sovereignty of the Grail itself or of its law
through an improper attitude to *Minne,* or love."[2]

Like Parsifal and the king, we do not recognize the Grail
within us. We must open our eyes and expand our consciousness. We need the moist, juicy, green, caring feminine to heal
the wounded, dry, brittle, overextended masculine in our
culture. Otherwise we inhabit a wasteland. Parsifal had the
experience of the Grail, the Grail Castle, and the wounded
Fisher King, but he did not ask "What ails thee?" If we are to
heal, we must make the question conscious. The unrelated,
out-of-control, masculine element within each one of us drives
us beyond a point of balance. It is like the oil tanker *Valdez*
careening off course, running aground, and befouling Mother
Nature.

The Unrelated Masculine

A crazy unknown force
rams Our Mother with a drunken boat
the thick black sludge penetrates Her skin
it enters my dreams
contaminates our consciousness
we are all drunk on oil

we dull our senses
divert our eyes
look for scapegoats
scour her beaches
clean her birds
cage her otters
deny our interconnection
we'll befoul Her again

I ache for Mother Earth
ignored
taken advantage of
Her riches mined for all
they are worth
humankind's greed and arrogance
desecrates
dirties
and
defiles
Her body

When will we learn
we are wounding our Mother
everything we do
affects everyone else
we can no longer ignore
we are trees sea and earth
we must make Her safe
from our excess

I have just returned (May 25, 1989) from Valdez, Alaska, where I was working with children suffering from the after-effects of the oil spill on their lives, and I have been asking myself the question left unasked by Parsifal. I was stunned by the level of denial on the part of oil company spokespeople about the effect of the sludge on the ecosystem, the lives of the animals, and the life style of the people who live in the affected fishing villages. "We'll have this spill cleaned up by September 15, 1989." . . . "There aren't that many dead animals." . . . "There weren't any people killed, so why you are leading grief groups?"

They lie, obfuscate, and deny the massive destruction to the environment. They exhibit little compassion for the loss of fishermen's livelihood or the painful deaths experienced by sea birds and otters. There is a massive public relations effort to minimize the toxic effects of 240,000 barrels of runaway oil. Exxon and the Alaska Tourist Board have mounted a four-million-dollar advertising campaign using the image of Marilyn Monroe without her beauty mark to dispel the fear that Alaska's beauty has been marred. "Unless you look long and hard, you probably won't notice her beauty mark is missing," reads the ad. "Without it, the picture may have changed, but her beauty hasn't. The same is true of Alaska. The oil spill may have temporarily changed a small part of the picture, but the things you come here to see and do are as beautiful as ever."[3]

This type of egregious denial is an example of the unrelated, wounded, dangerous masculine holding onto its perception of reality. There is an element of this within each one of us. We are blind to the rigid, driven, dominating masculine that controls our psyche. Each time we deny our feelings, body, dreams, and intuition we serve this inner tyrant.

The only way a woman can heal this imbalance within herself is to bring the light of consciousness into the darkness. She must be willing to face and name her shadow tyrant and let it go. This requires a conscious sacrifice of mindless attachments to ego power, financial gain, and hypnotic, passive living. It takes courage, compassion, humility, and time.

The challenge for the heroine is not one of conquest but one of acceptance, of accepting her nameless, unloved parts that have become tyrannical because she has left them unchecked. We can't go through life blindly. We have to examine all of the conflicting parts of ourselves. Each one of us has dragons lurking in the shadows. The challenge, according to Edward Whitmont, requires "the strength to sustain awareness and the suffering of conflict and to be able to surrender oneself to it."[4] It is the job of the heroine to enlighten the world by loving it—starting with herself.[5]

Releasing Machisma

In 1984 I had a dream on the night preceding a vision quest I co-led in the Santa Cruz Mountains. The dream voice said, "The return trip home to the feminine is when we release machisma." This cryptic message was the first time I had heard the term *machisma*, but I knew that it was a code for "I can tough it out; I'm strong; I don't need any help; I'm self-sufficient; I can do it alone," which is the voice of the stereotypical hero revered in this culture.

The dream voice carried the double-edged humor of the trickster because the morning brought rain and we began our hike of twenty-six miles in a downpour that lasted four days. Because of the continuous wet and my lack of adequate protective gear, I needed to call upon all the strength and stamina I could muster. But I understood that the voice was urging me to let go of the "lone ranger" warrior archetype.

There comes a point in each woman's life when she is faced with a particular choice about being a woman. She may be presented with a dilemma about relationship, career, motherhood, friendship, illness, aging, or the transition of mid-life. For one brief moment—or month or year—she is given the opportunity that was presented so long ago to Parsifal: the opportunity to be *in* a situation, to assess it, and to ask, "What ails me?"

If she has wittingly or unwittingly chosen the path of the masculine warrior, she can either continue stoically along this path alone, fine-tuning her identity and learning the breadth and width of power and acclaim in the world, or she can internalize the skills learned on the hero's journey and integrate these with the wisdom of her feminine nature.

There is no doubt that she needs the masculine: "the unconscious cannot carry out the process of individuation on its own; it is dependent on the cooperation of consciousness. This needs a strong ego."[6] But she needs a relationship with the *positive* inner masculine, the Man with Heart. He will support her with compassion and strength to heal her tired ego and reclaim her deep feminine wisdom. For this positive man with heart to emerge she needs to honor her feminine nature.

The Sacred Marriage

Through the sacred marriage, the *hieros gamos*, the unity of all opposites, woman remembers her true nature. "It is a moment of recognition, a kind of remembering of that which somewhere at bottom we have always known. The current problems are not solved, the conflicts remain, but such a person's suffering, as long as [s]he does not evade it, will no longer lead to neuroses but to new life. The individual intuitively glimpses who [s]he is."[7]

The sacred marriage is the marriage of ego and self. The heroine comes to understand the dynamics of her feminine and masculine nature and accepts them both together. June Singer writes:

> A wise person once said that the goal of the masculine principle is perfection and the goal of the feminine principle is completion. If you are perfect, you cannot be complete, because you must leave out all the imperfections of your nature. If you are complete, you cannot be perfect, for being complete means that you contain good and evil, right and wrong, hope and despair. So perhaps it is best to be content with something less than perfection and something less than completion. Perhaps we need to be more willing to accept life as it comes.[8]

The result of this union is the "birth of the divine child." A woman gives birth to herself as a divine androgenous being, autonomous, and in a state of perfection in the unity of the opposites. She is whole. Erich Neumann writes about this in

Lady Ragnell and Gawain

Amor and Psyche: The Psychic Development of the Feminine: "The birth of the 'divine child' and its significance are known to us from mythology, but even more fully from what we have learned of the individuation process. While to a woman the birth of the divine son signifies a renewal and deification of her animus-spirit aspect, the birth of the divine daughter represents a still more central process, relevant to woman's self and wholeness."[9] In the union of Spirit (Psyche) and love (Amor) a sacred daughter is born to them who is called Pleasure-Joy-Bliss. So too the sacred marriage conjoins the opposites, giving birth to ecstatic wholeness.

A Woman of Wisdom and a Man with Heart

The English tale "Gawain and Lady Ragnell" portrays the healing of both the wounded masculine and the distorted feminine. It joins the Woman of Wisdom with the Man with Heart. In *The Maid of the North* Ethel Johnson Phelps recounts this story, which takes place in the fourteenth-century English countryside.[10]

One day in late summer Gawain, the nephew of King Arthur, was with his uncle and the knights of the court at Carlisle. The king returned from the day's hunting in Inglewood looking so pale and shaken that Gawain followed him to his chamber and asked him what was the matter.

While out hunting alone, Arthur had been accosted by a fearsome knight of the northern lands named Sir Gromer who sought revenge for the loss of his lands. He spared Arthur, giving him the chance to save his life by meeting him in a year at the same spot, unarmed, with the answer to the question:

"What is it that women most desire, above all else?" If he found
the correct answer to this question his life would be spared.

Gawain assured Arthur that together they would be able to
find the correct answer to the question, and during the next
twelve months they collected answers from one corner of the
kingdom to the other. As the day drew near, Arthur was
worried that none of the answers had the ring of truth.

A few days before he was to meet Sir Gromer, Arthur rode
out alone through the golden gorse and purple heather to a
grove of great oaks. There before him was a huge, grotesque
woman. "She was almost as wide as she was high, her skin was
mottled green and spikes of weedlike hair covered her head.
Her face seemed more animal than human."[11] Her name was
Lady Ragnell.

The woman told Arthur that she knew he was about to meet
her stepbrother, Sir Gromer, and that he did not have the
right answer to the question. She told him that she knew the
correct answer and would tell him if the knight Gawain would
become her husband. Arthur was shocked and cried out that
it was impossible; he could not give her his nephew.

"I did not ask you to give me the knight Gawain," she
rebuked him. "If Gawain himself agrees to marry me, I will
give you the answer. Those are my terms."[12] She told him that
she would meet him at the same spot the next day, and she
disappeared into the oak grove.

Arthur was crestfallen because he could not consider asking
his nephew to give his own life in marriage to this ugly woman
in order to save himself. Gawain rode out from the castle to
meet the king, and when he saw him looking pale and strained
he asked Arthur what had happened. At first Arthur declined
to tell him, but when he finally told Gawain the terms of Lady
Ragnell's proposal, Gawain was delighted that he would be
able to save Arthur's life. When Arthur pleaded with him not
to sacrifice himself, Gawain answered, 'It is my choice and my
decision. I will return with you tomorrow and agree to the
marriage—on condition that the answer she supplies is the
right one to save your life."[13]

Arthur and Gawain met the Lady Ragnell and agreed to her

conditions. The following day Arthur rode alone, unarmed, to Inglewood to meet Sir Gromer. Arthur first tried all of his other answers, and just as Sir Gromer lifted his sword to cleave Arthur in two, Arthur added, "I have one more answer. What a woman desires above all else is the power of sovereignty— the right to exercise her own will."[14] Sir Gromer, angered because he knew that Arthur must have learned the true answer from Lady Ragnell, swore an oath against his stepsister and ran off into the forest.

Gawain held to his promise and married Lady Ragnell that day. After the wedding feast, which was attended in shock and uneasy silence by the knights and ladies of Arthur's court, the married couple retired to their chamber. The Lady Ragnell asked Gawain to kiss her. "Gawain went to her at once and kissed her. When he stepped back, there stood before him a slender young woman with gray eyes and a serene, smiling face."[15]

Gawain was shocked and wary of her sorcery and asked what had happened to effect such a dramatic change. She told him that her stepbrother had always hated her and had told his mother, who had a knowledge of sorcery, to change her into a monstrous creature who could only be released if the greatest knight in Britain willingly chose her for his bride. Gawain asked her why Sir Gromer hated her so.

"He thought me bold and unwomanly because I defied him. I refused his commands both for my property and my person."[16] Gawain smiled at her in admiration and marveled that the spell was now broken. "Only in part," she replied. "You have a choice, my dear Gawain, which way I will be. Would you have me in this, my own shape, at night and my former ugly shape by day? Or would you have me grotesque at night in our chamber, and my own shape in the castle by day? Think carefully before you choose."[17]

Gawain thought for a moment and knelt before her, touched her hand, and told her it was a choice that he could not make because it was her choice only to make. He told her that whatever she chose he would willingly support. Ragnell radiated her joy. "You have answered well, dearest Gawain, for your answer has broken Gromer's evil spell completely. The last condition he set has been met! For he said that if, after marriage to the greatest knight in Britain, my husband freely gave me the power of choice, the power to exercise my own free will, the wicked enchantment would be broken forever."[18]

Lady Ragnell and Gawain were united in a sacred marriage of two equals who had made a free and conscious choice to come together. Lady Ragnell had been bewitched by her wicked stepbrother for asserting her will and protecting her sexuality, and the compassionate Gawain gave her the freedom to transform her disfiguration. She had the ability to save the king, and Gawain had the wisdom to recognize the sovereignty of the feminine. Together they found healing love. In some versions of the legend, the Lady Ragnell is the Grail Goddess, and Gawain is both her healer and lover.

Edward Whitmont writes, "The grail goddess is the heroine of a seasonal abduction story, mistress of the moon and vegetation, who transforms herself from the most hideous animal forms into radiant beauty and is a guide to the other world."[19] There is evidence from the Welsh version of this tale that Gawain is Parsifal's original name, so both Gawain and Parsifal are initiated into the mysteries of the feminine. Through reverence for the sovereignty of the Goddess in her repellant form, man is once again able to drink of her ever-flowing waters.[20] "In drinking of the Goddess's waters the ego's personal claim to power is renounced. Indeed, the ego acknowledges itself as but a recipient and channel of a destiny flowing from a deep, mysterious ground of being which is the source both of terror and revulsion as well as the beautiful play of life."[21]

Healing Powers of the Feminine: Hildegard

In the legend of the Holy Grail, Parsifal wanders for five years through the wasteland after failing to ask the correct question. After many trials and adventures, he returns to the castle of the Fisher King, and this time he asks the prescribed question, which heals the king. Once healed, the king is permitted to

die, and the wasteland is restored to fertility. Like Parsifal, we
are now being given the opportunity to recognize the need for
the healing feminine in our culture. If we ignore her this time,
we will truly have a nuclear wasteland.

Hildegard of Bingen, who was a twelfth-century abbess,
mystic, prophet, preacher, teacher, organizer, reformer, com-
poser, artist, healer, poet, and writer who lived in the lush
Rhineland Valley, said that the major sin of humanity is
aridness and its major need is to bring moisture and greenness
back into people's lives. Jean Shinoda Bolen, in speaking of
the applicability of Hildegard to the teachings of the Grail
says:

> Moisture and greenness have to do with innocence, love,
> heart, feelings and tears. All of the [fluids] in our body
> become moist when we are moved—we cry, we lubricate,
> we bleed; all of the numinous experiences of our bodies
> have to do with moisture. And it's moisture that brings
> life to this planet, that is the cure for the desert experi-
> ence and the cure for aridness. . . . We really will become
> arid if we cut down our rainforests. . . . We as a people
> need to be like Parsifal searching through that forest
> wilderness to return to the grail castle once more and to
> have the grail experience and know the meaning of it. We
> just get glimpses of it but that is a lot. [22]

Moisture brings healing to those who are dry. A dear friend
of mine, Steve, who was an educator with an enormous heart,
just died of AIDS. In his last days he imaged death as a relief
from the dryness of his deteriorating body, wasted inside and
out by Kaposi's sarcoma. He told me he was ready to go and
asked me what his passage would be like. "You're going to walk
weightless in a beautiful green meadow," I said. "It will be
lush, green, fertile, healing, and moist."

He smiled. "I'm so dry," he said. "Just let it be moist."

Dreaming of the Sacred Union

When a woman has the experience of the sacred marriage
within, she traditionally dreams of meeting the primal father,

a man more godlike than human; or she is led into the sacred marriage bed of a heavenly youth. She dreams of the wedding ceremony, her wedding dress or veil, the nuptial rites, and the bed of consummation. She sees the image of her wedding slipper or the sacred feast.

Her lover may take the form of a beast or a powerful male animal ally with whom she unites in strength and sensuality. One woman dreams repreatedly of making love with the lion Aslan from C. S. Lewis's *Narnia Chronicles* while a female bear stands witness to sanction their union.

A woman in her mid-forties dreams of a lover with whom she was engaged twenty years before. "I am swimming nude in the warm ocean waves under the stars, and he comes to me and embraces me. I am completely open to him and he to me. He leads me out of the sea and tenderly dries my body and wraps me in a white silk kimono. He takes my hand and leads me up into the mountain. The starlight illumines hundreds of miniature plants and flowers, each one a jewel. We walk through the meadow toward a doe in the distance. She is waiting for me; she is an ancient one, wise and loving."

C. S. Lewis created Aslan as the embodiment of the Christ consciousness. The bear and deer are both ancient symbols of the Mother Goddess. Both women dream of union with principles of the divine.

Many women today are finding their beloved in the Goddess. In "Uncursing the Dark" Betty DeShong Meador writes of the many forms in which the Goddess appears, often in times of deprivation and despair:

> She is a group of hungry hags in the molten center of the earth. She is a black woman who arrives to make love to the dreamer. She is a trollop, a whore; she is uncouth, brassy, cheap. She is a priestess leading an initiation in a room of fire. She is seductive, desiring the dreamer, awakening in her erotic love for a woman. She is a spring which wells up unexpectedly. She is animal. She is a long-buried pit being dug up. She is a wild cat feeding her young on a woman's lap. She is a swarm of bees rising out of an old record player. [23]

While writing this chapter I had the following dream. "I am lying with a woman. I am surprised to find myself with her because I have never been with a woman before. She is thin, smooth-skinned, and has small breasts. Her skin is almost transparent. She allows me to touch her and to kiss her nipples. She is open and available. I love her skin and the warmth of her body, so gentle. I lie there prone on her belly and become so aroused that my entire being begins to shake. I have a full body orgasm from my toes to the top of my head. It wakes me up. She reminds me of Isis bringing Osiris back to life." After having this dream I felt energized for the rest of the day, as well as deeply sensual and alive. I knew this was an important dream about tapping into Eros.

Many women poets express their erotic nature in its many facets, both sensual and spiritual. In "Ave" Diane Di Prima writes of her union with the divine feminine.

> . . . you are the hills, the shape and color of mesa
> you are the tent, the lodge of skins, the hogan
> the buffalo robes, the quilt, the knitted afghan
> you are the cauldron and the evening star
> you rise over the sea, you ride the dark
> I move within you, light the evening fire
> I dip my hand in you and eat your flesh
> you are my mirror image and my sister
> you disappear like smoke on mist hills
> you lead me thru dream forest on horseback
> large gypsy mother, I lean my head on your back
>
> > I am you
> > and I must become you
> > I have seen you
> > and I must become you
> > I am always you
> > I must become you . . . [24]

The sacred marriage is complete when a woman joins the two aspects of her nature. Anne Waldman, a poet and practicing Buddhist, says, "I need to join the woman principle (prajna) in the man in me with the man principle (upaya) in me." She goes on to say that we all need to breathe more knowledge,

more *prajna* into the world to restore the imbalance. She quotes
the contemporary Turkish poet Gulten Akin who writes:

> Living with people, as they live
> Inhaling the air they breathe
> Breathing knowledge into them[25]

This truly is the task of the contemporary heroine. She
heals as she breathes as she recognizes her true nature,
breathing knowledge into all of us. The heroine becomes the
Mistress of Both Worlds; she can navigate the waters of daily
life and listen to the teachings of the depths. She is the
Mistress of Heaven and Earth and of the Underworld. She has
gained wisdom from her experiences: she no longer needs to
blame the other; she *is* the other. She brings that wisdom back
to share with the world. And the women, men, and children
of the world are transformed by her journey.

10

Beyond Duality

Everyone is partly their ancestors;
just as everyone is
partly man and partly woman.
                    Virginia Woolf

The problem with you
Is the problem with me
The problem thinking we're so different
The problem is how to perceive . . .
            Anne Waldman, "Duality (A Song)"

We live in a dualistic culture which values, creates, and sustains polarities—an either/or stratified mentality which identifies and locates ideas and people at opposite ends of a spectrum. In writing about "creation spirituality," Matthew Fox explains in *Original Blessing* that the sin behind all sin is dualism: separation from self, separation from the divine, separation of me from you, separation of good from evil, separation of the sacred from nature. In dualistic thinking, we treat the other as an object outside of ourselves, some *thing* to better, to control, to distrust, to dominate, or to own. Dualism breeds suspicion, confusion, misperception, contempt, a lack of trust.

The sin of dualism mars our psyche, contaminating our attitudes about mind, body, soul; women, men, children; animals, nature, spirituality; as well as about political structures. We divide ideas and people into hierarchies of good/bad, us/them, black/white, right/wrong. We separate spirit from matter, mind from body, science from art, good from evil, life from death, women from men, fat from thin, young

from old, socialist from capitalist, and liberal from conservative. We see the other as the enemy, and we rationalize our
criticism, judgment, and the polarization we create by arro-
gantly saying that we are "correct" or that we have God or the
Goddess on our side.

This type of polarization has kept some people poor,
ignorant, or infirm while enabling others to be rich, well-
tended, and powerful. It has allowed nationalities to assert
their supremacy over people whose religious beliefs or view of
reality they disdain. It has allowed feminists to blame men for
the imbalance on the planet without taking responsibility for
their own desire for control and greed. It has given men
freedom from the excruciating self-examination required for
change, while they demand that women do all of their emotional work for them. It has supplied the powerful with
permission to suppress and distort knowledge, censor speech,
sterilize the "unfit," and cause incredible suffering over all the
planet. Human arrogance fails to see that *we are all one* and
coexist along a continuum of life.

Polarization leads one to view the other as an "it." The
philosopher Martin Buber describes the conflicting ways human beings view themselves and others in his book *I and Thou*.
He describes two attitudes: that of I–It and that of I–Thou.
The I–It attitude treats the other as a *thing* that is separate from
self, to be measured, organized, and controlled; the I–It
attitude does not recognize the other as sacred. The I–Thou
attitude addresses the other as one and the same as self.[1]

Buber says that Thou cannot be controlled or found by
seeking; we meet Thou through grace, in mystery. Thou is an
experience of the sacred. If I address you as "Thou" instead of
as "It," whether you are human, animal, rock, or ocean, and if
I honor my own divinity, then I will honor the sacred within
you and allow you to live your life in trust, without coercion
or control by me.

Vietnamese Buddhist teacher Thich Nhat Hanh teaches that
there can be no duality, no separate self. We are all interconnected; we *inter-be*. To inter-be with something, or to be *one*

with something, we have to understand it; we have to enter into it. We cannot stand outside and observe it.

> You cannot just be by yourself alone. You have to *inter-be* with every other thing. This sheet of paper is, because everything else is. If you look into this sheet of paper you will see clearly that there is a cloud floating in it. Without a cloud, there can be no rain; without rain, the trees cannot grow; and without trees, we cannot make paper. The cloud is essential for the paper to exist. If the cloud is not here, the sheet of paper cannot be here either. So we can say that the cloud and the paper *inter-are*. Form is empty of a separate self, but it is full of everything in the cosmos. [2]

He goes on to explain that duality is an illusion. "There is right and there is left; if you take sides you are trying to eliminate half of reality which is impossible. It is an illusion to think you can have right without left, good without evil, women without men, the rose without the garbage, the United States without the Soviet Union." [3]

Healing the Split between Feminine and Masculine

The split between women and men may have its roots in property rights and procreation, but this split has been widened and reinforced by most religious and political systems. Genesis 3:16, which states that men should rule over women, was not a divine decree but a piece of patriarchal propaganda. Western religion has encouraged mankind to blame womankind for the evils of the world and to exclude women from having an equal voice in spiritual, political, and economic matters. Original sin, based on the fall of Adam and Eve in the Garden of Eden, has played an important role since the time of Augustine in the fourth century because, as Matthew Fox writes, "it plays kindly into the hands of empire-builders, slave masters and patriarchal society in general. It divides and thereby conquers, pitting one's thoughts against one's feelings, one's body against one's spirit, one's political vocation against personal needs, people against the earth, animals and nature in general." [4]

While researching her book *Adam, Eve and the Serpent*, Elaine Pagels was struck by "how deeply religious traditions are embedded in the structure of our political life and our institutions and our attitudes about human nature" and how deeply these affect our moral choices.[5] If the prevailing religious tradition is one that states that only God and the emperor, who is the representative of God on earth, are supreme, then it will be impossible for every person to make her own moral choice about how to live her life. These choices will have to be legislated for her. We see the existence of this mistrust in the present political turmoil over women's choice about bearing children.

If the prevalent attitude about human nature is one of sin and depravity, then there is no trust. There is also little room to allow for a change in attitude about one's enemies. Many politicians today exhibit this mentality in dealing with the Soviet Union. In response to criticism about the United States's delay in negotiating an end to the arms race, officials revert to the Cold War mentality, which says that the Soviets are only trying to trick us into reducing our defenses so that they can overcome our military might. According to this mentality trust in the "other" is considered ignorant, naive, or a sign of weakness.

Christ's message that every human being—woman, man, and child—was made in the image of God was very radical for the culture in which he lived. In the Roman Empire three-fourths of the people were slaves or descended from slaves, and he preached that these people, not solely the emperor, were one with God.[6] This union of divinity and humanity had far-reaching political ramifications, and that is why Christ was put to death.

In patriarchal relationships, whether political, religious, or personal, only one person can be on the top; so there is always a controller and a controllee. For the dominant personality to retain power, she or he needs to keep her partner in a one-down position. This creates a particular mind-set in which one person expects to be in control and the other person expects to be controlled. There is a spatial model for this type of arrangement: when it involves two entities it looks like a see-saw; when it involves three or more it looks like a pyramid.[7]

In most work situations there is a boss who dominates the vision and thinking of the company and hires competent associates, who in turn quickly learn how to anticipate what the boss wants. Most families employ the pyramid structure as well: one adult dominates and the partner and/or children learn how to accommodate the needs, orders, and moods of the dominant adult. Sometimes, of course, the dominant person is a child who tyrannizes his or her parents. The army, the Catholic Church, most corporations, schools, and unions are prime examples of intractable, hierarchical pyramids. A school administrator in Los Angeles recently said of his faculty that it would be easier to move a cemetery than to get his teachers to cooperate with him.

Mary Ann Cejka writes about the sin of sexism which has created these hierarchical pyramids in our culture and traces the roots of these structures and resultant attitudes not to Christianity or Judaism but to the Roman Empire. She calls for a conversion from hierarchy to community.

> Marc Ellis of the Maryknoll School of Theology argues that the central calling of Christians today, both as Church and as individuals, is the call to conversion from empire to community. To be converted from empire is to dissociate ourselves from the pyramid. The structure of community is a circle. Movement within a circle takes place easily and not at the expense of others. The circle as a whole is the basic form of a wheel, and as such it is the appropriate social structure for a "pilgrim people," *a people on a journey together.* People within a circle share an equal perspective; they can look each other in the eye. The circle facilitates accountability.[8] (italics added)

A Circular Perspective

The circle is inclusive; it does not exclude. The symbol of the feminine is the circle, exemplified in the womb, the vessel, and the grail. Women tend to cluster; they like being related, helpful, and connected. They have always done things *together,* like sewing, quilting, pickling, and watching children in the park. They ask each other for support, and they celebrate each other's accomplishments. "Women have always met in circles—facing one another like colleagues, no one with authority or power 'over' the other."[9]

In *The Chalice and the Blade,* Riane Eisler draws from reports of recent archeological excavations by Marija Gimbutas to show that entire societies used to be based on the model of the circle or the chalice, rather than that of the pyramid or the blade.[10] These societies exemplified the partnership model of *power with* rather than the dominator model of *power over.* The Neolithic societies of Old Europe between 7000 and 3500 B.C.E. were civilizations that displayed complex religious and governmental institutions, used copper and gold for ornaments and tools, had a rudimentary script, and were sexually equalitarian. They were less authoritarian and more peaceful than hierarchic societies.

Sites in Catal Huyuk and Hacilar in Turkey showed no evidence, for a time span of over fifteen hundred years, of damage through warfare nor of male dominance: "the evidence indicates a generally unstratified and basically equalitarian society with no marked distinctions based on either class or sex."[11]

By looking at the placement of the contents of grave sites in practically all the known cemeteries of Old Europe, Marija Gimbutas concluded that an equalitarian male/female society existed in Neolithic times. She writes, "In the 53-grave cemetary of Vinca, hardly any difference in wealth of equipment was discernible between male and female graves. . . . In respect to the role of women in the society, the Vinca evidence suggests an equalitarian and clearly non-patriarchal society. The same can be adduced of the Varna society: I can see there no ranking along a patriarchal masculine-feminine value scale."[12]

There were indicators that these were matrilineal societies in which descent and inheritance were traced through the mother, and women played key roles in all aspects of life. "In the models of house-shrines and temples, and in actual temple remains females are shown supervising the preparation and performance of rituals dedicated to the various aspects and functions of the Goddess. Enormous energy was expended in the production of cult equipment and votive gifts. . . . The most sophisticated creations of Old Europe—the most exquisite vases, sculptures, etc. now extant—were woman's work."[13] The sculptures found in Paleolithic caves and in the open plains of Anatolia and other Near Eastern and Middle Eastern Neolithic sites show that the worship of the Goddess was central to all life. These sculptures indicate that the mythological images of the period's religious rites and feminine figures and symbols occupied a central place in the sites.[14]

Neolithic art shows a notable absence of weapons, heroes, battles, slavery, or military fortifications. These were not dominator societies. They were not yet touched by the later nomadic tribes of the Kurgan invasion which worshiped blood-thirsty gods. The Goddess was central to all aspects of life. Symbols of nature—sun, water, bulls, birds, fish, serpents, cosmic eggs, butterflies, and images of the Goddess both pregnant and giving birth—have been found everywhere in shrines and houses, on vases and clay figurines.[15] "And if the central religious image was a woman giving birth and not, as in our time, a man dying on a cross, it would not be unreasonable to infer that life and the love of life—rather than death and the fear of death—were dominant in society as well as art."[16]

In these societies there was no separation between the secular and the sacred; religion was life and life was religion. In the goddess religions, the head of the holy family was a woman: the Great Mother. In the secular family, descent was traced through the mother and the domicile was matrilocal; the husband went to live with his wife's clan or family.[17] This did not make it a matriarchy: both men and women were children of the Goddess and "neither half of humanity ranked over the other and diversity [was] not equated with inferiority or superiority."[18] The attitude that prevailed was one of linking rather than ranking, partnership rather than domination.

Gimbutas writes that "the world of myth was not polarized

into female and male as it was among the Indo-Europeans and many other nomadic and pastoral peoples of the steppes. Both principles were manifest side by side. The male divinity [that often accompanied the Goddess] in the shape of a young man or male animal appears to affirm and strengthen the forces of the creative and active female. Neither is subordinate to the other: by complementing one another, their power is doubled."[19]

There have been various times in the recorded history of humankind when partnership societies existed in which the life-giving aspects of the divine were worshiped as part of everyday life, and gender differences in carrying out religious and daily practices did not exist. We know these existed not only from Paleolithic cave art in western Europe and the burial chambers at Catal Huyuk and Hacilar, but also from what we know of Minoan Cretans, Gnostic Christians, early Celts, Native Americans, and Balinese, to name just a few.

Dual Nature of the Divine

Mircea Eliade has written about the dual nature of the divine existing in many religions where even the most supremely feminine or masculine divinities were androgynous. "Under whatever form the divinity manifests itself, he or she is ultimate reality, absolute power, and this reality, this power, will not let itself be limited by any attributes whatsoever (good, evil, male, female, or anything else)."[20]

In *Male/Female Language* Mary Ritchie Key writes that the Aztecs, who did not have a gender-based grammatical system, believed that the origin of the world and all human beings was a single principle with a dual nature. "This supreme being had a male and female countenance. . . . This god had the regenerating ability of both male and female. This dual deity, *Ometeotl,* had two different aspects of a single supreme being. *Ome* = two and *teotl* = god."[21]

Elaine Pagels writes about the Gnostic Gospels, the fifty-two texts written by early Christians in the first through fourth centuries A.D. which were discovered at Nag Hammadi in

Upper Egypt in 1945 by an Arab peasant. These heretical teachings present evidence that Jesus spoke of God the Mother and God the Father. In the Gospel of Thomas, Jesus contrasts his earthly parents, Mary and Joseph, with his divine mother, the Holy Spirit, and his divine father, the Father of Truth.[22] The Spirit is both Mother and Virgin, the consort and counterpart of the heavenly Father. In the Gospel of Philip, the mystery of the virgin birth of Christ refers to "that mysterious union of the two divine powers, the Father of All and the Holy Spirit."[23] In addition to the eternal, mystical Silence and the Holy Spirit, the divine mother was also characterized as Sophia: wisdom, the original thought. "Besides being the 'first universal creator,' who brings forth all creatures, she also enlightens human beings and makes them wise."[24]

By the year A.D. 200 virtually all feminine imagery for God had disappeared from the mainstream Christian tradition. Until that time, however, there is evidence that women held positions of power in the Church. "In such gnostic groups as the Valentinians, women were considered equal to men; some were revered as prophets, teachers, traveling evangelists, healers, priests and perhaps even bishops."[25] This was not universally applicable, but around A.D. 180 Clement of Alexandria, a revered father of the Egyptian church who identified himself as orthodox, but who had contact with Gnostic groups wrote, ". . . men and women share equally in perfection, and are to receive the same instruction and the same discipline. For the name 'humanity' is common to both men and women; and for us 'in Christ there is neither male nor female.' "[26]

Clement's equalitarian attitude unfortunately found little following among other second-century church leaders. The consciousness of the male hierarchy was not open to equality of women on either secular or theological grounds. "Whether creative possibilities or regressive destruction shall prevail depends not upon the nature of the archetype or myth, but upon the attitude and degree of consciousness."[27] Clement found that his perspective, which was formed in the cosmopolitan atmosphere of Alexandria among the educated and wealthy members of Egyptian society, had little impact on the

majority of Western Christian communities scattered throughout Asia Minor, Greece, Rome, provincial Africa, and Gaul.[28]

Celtic Christianity

The seed of early Christianity blossomed in different arenas
according to the culture in which it took root. The early Celts
were a tribal people whose whole society was oriented toward
an integration of spirituality and life. They believed all life
emanated from Source and the function of life was to live in
harmony with unseen realms. The triple spiral found in Celtic
art reflects the energy of the Triple Goddess: the causal world,
the world of thought (the mystical world), and the physical
world. Because the deity was found both in nature and in the
soul, the natural world was seen as the doorway to the unseen
realms.

Into this very fertile understanding of the mysteries came
the figure of Jesus, who knew how to go back and forth
between the two worlds. This capacity to live the Mystery, to
walk between the worlds, was already a part of Celtic consciousness, so the figure of Jesus was adopted with a passion at
Druidic centers of learning throughout the land of the Celts.
The Celtic cross never focused on the death of Christ, but on
the capacity to go back and forth between the worlds.

Instead of doctrine, Celtic Christianity emphasized the
direct individual experience of spirit. The people were encouraged to speak it and to live it, with soul friends as co-
counselors. The community was nonhierarchical; the soul
friend was primary as spiritual adviser, rather than the ecclesi-
astical authority of the bishops. Celtic Christianity embraced
the feminine, the development of intuition, and it encouraged
the sensual experience of life. Sensual emotion was considered
to be the wisdom of the body, and the human body could
never be considered evil. There was a tremendous emphasis
on learning and an understanding that through free will human
beings have the power to live within the design of nature.

Since the Celts were a tribal people, their social model

within the centers of learning was decentralized; authority resided within the group, and the abbess or abbot served the role of a skilled therapist. This is very similar to the workings of Zen Buddhism. The Celtic Christians believed that spirit manifested in a five-tiered interacting energy field with no hierarchy: the worlds of minerals, plants, animals, humans, and angels were interconnected.

This five-tiered energy field became a living reality to me while studying Celtic Christianity with Vivienne Hull on the Isle of Iona, Scotland. This beautiful island is a "very thin place," a place where it is easy to walk between the worlds, a place where one is consciously aware of being touched by the unseen realms.

In the Celtic Christian Church women held their place as equals beside men; women traveled as preachers throughout the British Isles and held positions of authority. St. Brigit was an abbess of Kildare in the fifth century who tended the sacred Beltane fire, as did eleven of her children. The fire continued to burn until the eleventh century, when the bishop extinguished it under directives from Rome. Despite censure by the Roman church, Celtic Christianity never lost its orientation to the feminine, nature, mysticism, and intuition. The Celtic Christians felt that when religion separates from the feminine, it separates from the earth. Celtic Christianity flourished for one thousand years and today is reflowering. It asks the question of us all: "Are we willing to be edge dwellers and to walk between the worlds?"[29]

The world currently faces many difficult transitions, and people of all countries are concerned about the planet as a whole and the well-being of the earth community. The need is urgent to restore spiritual vision in the very heart of our lives. As we approach the millenium, many of the ancient teachings that honor the interrelation of matter and spirit, body and mind, nature and the sacred, human and divine are returning. Mayan, Tibetan Buddhist, Native American, Creation spirituality, and Goddess religions are reviving these ancient truths.

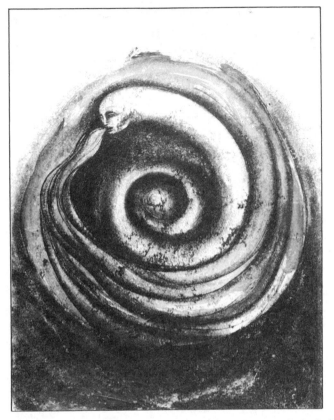

Birthstone. Painting by Deborah Koff-Chapin from *At the Pool of Wonder: Dreams and Visions of an Awakening.* Copyright © 1989 by Marcia Lauck and Deborah Koff-Chapin. Reproduced with permission of Bear & Company Publishing.

The Circle as a Model for Living

The purest, simplest, most encompassing form is the circle.[30] It is the first form that a child draws, a form repeated endlessly in nature. It has harmony, it gives comfort, it is transformative. A circle has no beginning and no end. "Nothing is excluded; everything finds its place and is understood as an integral aspect of a whole process."[31] When one sits in a circle with others, everyone is equal and linked. No one person is in power; the power is shared, and there is no place for egocentrism. Because everyone is interrelated and derives meaning only through the relationship of the circle, each person's vision is transformed as the circle takes form. Magic occurs in circles. A circle is a hug of giving and receiving; it teaches us about unconditional love.

"The primeval Mandala was doubtless a circle drawn upon the ground. Stepping forth from that circle, the initiate moved through a world of magic in which he was but a tongue of the earth chanting her song to the stars. The wheel of time returns. The magic circle is drawn once again."[32]

I recently had the opportunity to participate in a five-day retreat for high school seniors in which we used the Native American tribal council as the primary form of communication. In council we sit in a circle and pass a talking stick. Only the person holding this ritual object may talk, and the other members of the circle listen with their hearts. We enter ritual space and time.

The topic for council was male/female relationships, and we entered into a period of timeless time wherein each person's attitudes about this volatile subject were transformed. In the course of the exchange I realized that this circle was a powerful vehicle for women and men to change their attitudes about themselves and each other, to speak and to listen to each other with their hearts.

We heard the pain of an adolescent girl who was molested by her father and her resultant outrage at all males for not stopping the subtle and overt abuse of women. She held each male there responsible. The boys responded to her accusations with their own outrage and disgust about the insensitivity and abuse of certain males whose only power came at the expense of others. They also expressed their own fear and shame about not knowing how to intervene and their concern about being categorized as abusive males. Their feelings of inadequacy were palpable.

Girls voiced their anger about sexual harassment on the street and their feelings of fear for their safety. Boys discussed their insecurities about their physical bodies, having to live up to the macho male image in this culture, and their confusion about how to be with girls socially without being expected to perform sexually. Girls talked about how they were constantly judged in school for their bodies and appearance and how they needed to be more intelligent than their male classmates to get attention in class. Boys described the pain and frustration of listening to male friends brag about sexual exploits with girls who were their friends. Both girls and boys talked about the fear of separation from family and friends when they moved on after graduation.

There were many tears and many tense moments. Anger was expressed about the misperceptions people held about each other. Fear was expressed that women and men would never live together in harmony with so much confusion about each other, often held in silence. We heard the prejudices people carry about others of a different race, age, or sexual persuasion. It took four hours for twenty-six students and faculty to speak. You could hear a pin drop; attention was riveted on the person who held the talking stick. No one who left that circle remained unchanged.

That night I had a dream about our council in which a snake entered the door and slithered into the center of the circle. No one moved; we all watched the snake in silence. She circled the group and slowly peered at each person, stopping now and then to take a longer stare. She finally rested her eyes on me, looking deeply, perhaps even through me. She opened her mouth, and said one word, but she said it with such emphasis that I understood immediately. *"Transformation,"* she hissed.

This council gave me great hope. If high school students can come together in a circle with their elders and listen deeply to each person's fear, anger, joy, despair, and hope for the future, then perhaps these adolescents and the children who come after them will be able to effect a healing of the sin of duality. These children are learning compassion; they are learning to accept one another, to value caring and affiliation rather than conquest and domination. They are learning that we are all basically one and the same.

The compassion we experienced together will enable each

one of us to move closer to understanding diversity rather than being threatened by it. I believe that women are deeply affecting the critical mass. As each one of us heals our own feminine and masculine nature we change the consciousness on the planet from one of addiction to suffering, conflict, and domination to a consciousness that recognizes the need for affiliation, healing, balance, and *inter-being*. Women need to breathe more knowledge, more prajna, into the world to restore the imbalance. We *are* a pilgrim people; we are on a journey *together* to learn how to honor and preserve the dignity of all life forms seen and unseen; therein lies our heroic power.

Conclusion

The old story is over, and the myth of the heroic quest has taken a new turn on the evolutionary spiral. The quest for the "other," for title, attainment, acclaim, and riches, for one's fifteen seconds of fame in the news is no longer germane. That misguided quest has taken too much of a toll on the body/soul of woman and the cellular structure of Mother Earth.

Today's heroine must utilize the sword of discernment to cut away the ego bonds that hold her to the past and to find out what serves her soul's purpose. She must release resentment toward the mother, put aside blame and idolization of the father, and find the courage to face her own darkness. Her shadow is hers to name and embrace. Woman illumines these dark, shadowy spaces within her through the practice of meditation, art, poetry, play, ritual, relationship, and digging in the earth.

The word *heroine* has had many meanings, and the woman who has borne the title has worn many guises. She has been a damsel in distress waiting for rescue from the knight in shining armor, a Valkyrie riding on air leading her troops into battle, an artist alone painting bones in the desert, a tiny nun healing the wounds of the poor in Calcutta, and a supermom juggling briefcase and baby formula. She has changed the face of woman with each passing generation.

The task of today's heroine as we approach the millenium is to mine the silver and gold within her*self*. She must develop a positive relationship with her inner Man with Heart and find the voice of her Woman of Wisdom to heal her estrangement from the sacred feminine. As she honors her body and soul as well as her mind, she heals the split within herself and the culture. Women today are acquiring the courage to express their vision, the strength to set limits, and the willingness to take responsibility for themselves and others in a new way. They are reminding the people of their origins, the necessity to live mindfully, and their obligation to preserve life on earth.

Women are weavers; we intertwine with men, children and each other to protect the web of life.

Women are creators; we give birth to the young ones and to the children of our dreams.

Women are healers; we know the mysteries of the body, blood and spirit because they are one and the same.

Women are lovers; we joyfully embrace each other, men, children, animals and trees listening with our hearts to their triumphs and sorrows.

Women are alchemists; we uncover the roots of violence, destruction and desecration of the feminine and transform cultural wounds.

Women are the protectors of the soul of the Earth; we bring the darkness out of hiding and honor the unseen realms.

Women are divers; we move down into the Mysteries where it is safe and wondrous and oozing with new life.

Women are singers, dancers, prophets and poets; we call upon Mother Kali to help us remember who we are as we journey through life.

Kali, be with us.
Violence, destruction, receive our homage.
Help us to bring darkness into the light,
To lift out the pain, the anger,
Where it can be seen for what it is—
The balance-wheel for our vulnerable, aching love.
Put the wild hunger where it belongs,
Within the act of creation,
Crude power that forges a balance
Between hate and love.

Help us to be the always hopeful,
Gardeners of the spirit

Who know that without darkness
Nothing comes to birth
As without light
Nothing flowers.

Bear the roots in mind,
You, the dark one, Kali,
Awesome power. [1]

Notes

Introduction

1. Joseph Campbell, interview with author, New York, 15 September 1981.
2. Anne Truitt, *Daybook: The Journal of an Artist* (New York: Penguin Books, 1982), p. 110.
3. Joseph Campbell, *The Hero with a Thousand Faces*, p. 245.
4. Campbell interview.
5. Ibid.
6. Starhawk, *Dreaming the Dark*, p. 47.
7. Madeleine L'Engle, "Shake the Universe," pp. 182–85.
8. Rhett Kelly, "Lot's wife," 1989.

Chapter 1. Separation from the Feminine

1. Harriet Goldhor Lerner, *Women in Therapy*, p. 230.
2. Polly Young-Eisendrath and Florence Wiedemann, *Female Authority*, p. 4.
3. Joseph Campbell, *The Hero with a Thousand Faces*, p. 337.
4. The terms *feminine* and *masculine* are used to describe ways of being, inherent principles of human existence embodied by both women and men. They do not refer to gender. *Feminine* has been distorted by Western culture to convey woman/weakness, while *masculine* has been distorted to convey man/strength. These words should instead refer to a continuum of attributes inherent in all humans unlimited by gender. The woman's quest is to identify her ways of being for herself without the limitations imposed by words such as *feminine* and *masculine*.
5. Sibylle Birkauser-Oeri, *The Mother*, p. 14.
6. Lerner, *Women in Therapy*, p. 58.
7. Carol Pearson and Katherine Pope, *The Female Hero in American and British Literature*, p. 105.
8. Ibid.

9. Kathie Carlson, *In Her Image: The Unhealed Daughter's Search for Her Mother* (Boston & Shaftesbury: Shambhala Publications, 1989), p. 55.

10. Pearson and Pope, *The Female Hero*, p. 120.

11. Young-Eisendrath and Wiedemann, *Female Authority*, p. 45.

12. Ibid., p. 24.

13. Rich, *Of Woman Born*, pp. 246–47.

14. Barbara G. Walker, *The Woman's Encyclopedia of Myths and Secrets*, p. 488.

15. See Marija Gimbutas, *Goddesses and Gods of Ancient Europe*, and Merlin Stone, *When God Was a Woman*.

16. The term *matrophobia*, coined by poet Lynn Sukenick, is the fear not of being like one's mother but of becoming one's mother. See Rich, *Of Woman Born*, p. 237.

17. Rich, *Of Woman Born*, p. 218.

18. Lerner, *Women in Therapy*, p. 182.

19. Ibid.

20. Carol Pearson, *The Hero Within*, p. 196.

21. Cheri Gaulke, interview with author, Los Angeles, Calif., 23 October 1986.

22. Ibid.

23. According to a study by the Rand Corporation released in February 1989 and reported in "Women Narrowing Wage Gap, but Poverty Grows, Study Finds" (*Sacramento Bee Final*, 8 February 1989), wages for all working women increased from sixty to sixty-five percent of men's wages between 1980 and 1986. In the age range from twenty to twenty-four, women's wages increased from seventy-eight percent of men's wages to eighty-six percent. By the year 2000 the conservative estimate is that women will make seventy-four percent of men's wages. Poverty is a condition more likely experienced by women because of their lower wages and because most single-parent families are headed by mothers. In 1940, only one out of ten families had female heads of household. By 1980, however, this figure had increased by forty percent. Women headed almost one in seven families. Sixty-two percent of poor adults were women. The difference in men's and women's earning capacities did not cause sex-differentiation in poverty statistics as long as families remained intact. That protection ended with the rising incidence of divorce and unwed parenting and the resulting proliferation of single-parent families.

In a study of working parents and the revolution at home published in *The Second Shift* (New York: Viking, 1989), sociologist Arlie Hochschild found that women perform the majority of household tasks and do most of the parenting, trying in effect to perform two full-time jobs in one twenty-four-hour day. According to her computations compiled over an eight-year period, she found that on average American women in the past two decades have worked roughly fifteen hours longer each week than men. Over a year that adds up to an extra month of twenty-four-hour days. Only women who earned more than their husbands did less than half the housework.

24. Janet O. Dallett, *When the Spirits Come Back*, p. 27.
25. Young-Eisendrath and Wiedemann, *Female Authority*, p. 63.
26. Carlson, *In Her Image*, p. 77.

Chapter 2. Identification with the Masculine

1. Linda Schmidt, "How the Father's Daughter Found Her Mother," p. 8.
2. Kathy Mackay, "How Fathers Influence Daughters," pp. 1–2.
3. Ibid.
4. Ibid.
5. Ibid.
6. Ibid.
7. Ibid.
8. Linda Leonard, *The Wounded Woman*, pp. 113–14.
9. Mackay, "How Fathers Influence Daughters."
10. Jean Shinoda Bolen, *Goddesses in Everywoman*, p. 7.
11. "Making It," *L.A. Times Magazine*, Dec. 4, 1988, p. 72.
12. Polly Young-Eisendrath and Florence Wiedemann, *Female Authority*, p. 49.
13. Carol Pearson and Katherine Pope, *The Female Hero in American and British Literature*, p. 121.
14. Lewis Carroll, *Alice's Adventures in Wonderland and Through the Looking Glass*, p. 165.
15. Pearson and Pope, *The Female Hero*, p. 123.
16. Linda Schierse Leonard, *The Wounded Woman*, p. 17.
17. Mackay, "How Fathers Influence Daughters."
18. Carol Pearson, *The Hero Within*, p. 125–26.

Chapter 3. The Road of Trials

1. Kathy Mackay, "How Fathers Influence Daughters."
2. Harriet Goldhor Lerner, *Women in Therapy*, p. 159.
3. Ibid., p. 162.
4. Betty Friedan, *The Second Stage*, p. 219.
5. Carol Pearson and Katherine Pope, *The Female Hero in American and British Literature*, p. 66.

6. Ibid., p. 255.
7. Polly Young-Eisendrath and Florence Wiedemann, *Female Authority*, p. 119.
8. Pearson and Pope, *The Female Hero*, p. 143.
9. The story of Psyche and Eros is taken from Robert A. Johnson, *She: Understanding Feminine Psychology*, pp. 5–22.
10. Johnson, *She*, p. 23.
11. Ibid., p. 69.

Chapter 4. The Illusory Boon of Success

1. "Making It," *L.A. Times Magazine*, 4 December 1988, pp. 72–74.
2. Betty Friedan, *The Second Stage*, p. 56.
3. Ibid., p. 113.
4. Helen M. Luke, *Woman, Earth and Spirit*, p. 8.
5. Madonna Kolbenschlag, *Kiss Sleeping Beauty Goodbye*, p. 83.

Chapter 5. Strong Women Can Say No

1. Quoted in "Fueling the Inner Fire: A Conversation with Marti Glenn," *Venus Rising*, 3, no. 1 (1989).
2. Roger L. Green, *Heroes of Greece and Troy*, p. 222.
3. Ibid., pp. 222–23.
4. Carol P. Christ, *Laughter of Aphrodite*, pp. 97–98.
5. Ibid., pp. 98–99.
6. Ibid., p. 99.
7. John Russell, *New York Times*, "Arts and Leisure" section, February 1981. Cited in Betty Friedan, *The Second Stage*.
8. Excerpts from a workshop with Jean Shinoda Bolen in "The Journey of the Heroine," *Venus Rising*, 3, no. 1 (1989).
9. Sylvia Brinton Perera, *Descent to the Goddess*, p. 8.

Chapter 6. The Initiation and Descent to the Goddess

1. Patricia Reis, "The Goddess and the Creative Process," in Patrice Wynne, *The Womanspirit Sourcebook*, p. 181.
2. Barbara Walker, *The Skeptical Feminist*, p. 117.
3. Ibid., p. 122.
4. Merlin Stone, *When God Was a Woman*, p. 219.
5. Barbara Walker, *The Skeptical Feminist*, p. 133.
6. Barbara Walker, *The Woman's Encyclopedia of Myths and Secrets*, pp. 218–19.
7. Ibid., p. 219–20.
8. Ibid., p. 220.

9. Charles Boer, trans., "The Hymn to Demeter," *Homeric Hymns*, 2nd ed. rev. (Texas: Irving, 1979), pp. 89–135.
10. Jean Shinoda Bolen, *Goddesses in Every Woman*, pp. 169–71.
11. Helen Luke, *Woman, Earth and Spirit*, p. 56.
12. Christine Downing, *The Goddess*, p. 48.
13. Luke, *Woman, Earth and Spirit*, p. 65.
14. C. G. Jung, "Psychological Aspects of the Kore," in Jung & Kerenyi, *Essays on a Science of Mythology*, p. 215.
15. Luke, *Woman, Earth and Spirit*, p. 57.
16. Ibid., p. 54.
17. Ibid., p. 64.
18. Sylvia Brinton Perera, *Descent to the Goddess*, pp. 9–10.
19. Ibid., p. 59.
20. Ibid., p. 23.
21. Ibid., p. 24.
22. Ibid., p. 40.
23. Ibid., p. 67.
24. Ibid., p. 70.
25. Ibid., p. 78.
26. Ibid., p. 81.
27. Ibid., p. 90.
28. Ibid., p. 94.
29. Ibid., p. 91.

Chapter 7. Urgent Yearning to Reconnect with the Feminine

1. Jean Shinoda Bolen, "Intersection of the Timeless with Time: Where Two Worlds Come Together," Address to Annual ATP Conference, Monterey, Calif., 6 August 1988.
2. Carol Christ, *Laughter of Aphrodite*, p. 124.
3. Bolen, ATP.
4. Jean Markale, *Women of the Celts*, p. 99.
5. Ibid., p. 99.
6. Ibid., p. 96.
7. Buffie Johnson, *Lady of the Beasts*, p. 262.
8. Markale, *Women of the Celts*, p. 100.
9. John Sharkey, *Celtic Mysteries*, p. 8.
10. Marion Woodman, *The Pregnant Virgin*, p. 58.
11. Ibid.
12. In Maureen Murdock, "Changing Women," p. 43.
13. Marie-Louise von Franz and James Hillman, *Jung's Typology*, p. 116.
14. P. L. Travers, "Out of Eden," p. 16.
15. Vietnamese Buddhist monk, Thich Nhat Hahn, teaches the simple meditation of breathing and smiling.

16. Sheila Moon, *Changing Woman and Her Sisters*, p. 139.
17. Ibid., pp. 136–38.
18. Ibid., p. 138.
19. Colleen Kelly, interview with author, Point Reyes, Calif., 1 November 1986.
20. Mina Klein and Arthur Klein, *Käthe Kollwitz*, p. 104.
21. Ibid., p. 82.
22. Ibid., p. 92.
23. Luisah Teish, interview with author, Los Angeles, Calif., 7 November 1986.
24. Moon, *Changing Woman*, pp. 157–58.
25. Ibid., p. 169.
26. Kathleen Jenks, "Changing Woman," p. 209, quoted from Klah, Hasten and Wheelwright, Mary, *Navajo Creation Myths* (Santa Fe, N.M.: Museum of Navajo Ceremonial Art, 1942), p. 152.
27. Joan Sutherland, interview with author, Malibu, Calif., 6 February 1986.
28. Murdock, "Changing Women," p. 44.
29. Nancee Redmond, untitled, 10 December 1986.

Chapter 8. *Healing the Mother/Daughter Split*

1. Janet Dallett, *When the Spirit Comes Back*, p. 32.
2. James Hillman and Marie-Louise von Franz, *Jung's Typology*, pp. 113–14.
3. Ibid.
4. Rose-Emily Rothenburg, "The Orphan Archetype."
5. Lynda W. Schmidt, "How the Father's Daughter Found Her Mother," p. 10.
6. Ibid., p. 18.
7. Patricia C. Fleming, "Persephone's Search for Her Mother," p. 143.
8. Ibid., pp. 144–47.
9. Ginette Paris, *Pagan Meditations*, p. 167.
10. Ibid., p. 178.
11. For information about women's gatherings, see Patrice Wynne, *The Womanspirit Sourcebook* (San Francisco: Harper & Row, 1988). For information about women's vision quests contact Shanja Kirstann, 58 Ramona, Oakland, Calif. 94611.
12. Paris, *Pagan Meditations*, p. 175.
13. Flor Fernandez, interview with author, Venice, Calif., 14 October 1989.
14. Mark Schorer, "The Necessity of Myth," in Henry A. Murray, ed., *Myth and Mythmaking*, p. 355.

15. Hilary Robinson, ed., *Visibly Female: Feminism and Art Today* (New York: Universe Books, 1988), p. 158.
16. Estella Lauter, *Women As Mythmakers*, p. 170.
17. Ibid., p. 1.
18. Ibid.
19. Nancy Ann Jones, interview with author, Los Angeles, Calif., 10 August 1988.
20. Ibid.
21. Mayumi Oda, interview with author partially quoted in Murdock, "Changing Woman," p. 45.
22. Ibid.
23. Buffie Johnson, interview with author, Venice, Calif., February 18, 1986.
24. Ibid.
25. Susan Griffin, "This Earth: What She Is to Me," *Woman and Nature*, p. 219.
26. Marion Woodman, *The Pregnant Virgin*, p. 10.

Chapter 9. Finding the Inner Man with Heart

1. Jean Shinoda Bolen, "Intersection of the Timeless with Time: Where Two Worlds Come Together," Address to Annual ATP Conference, Monterey, Calif., 6 August 1988.
2. Edward C. Whitmont. *Return of the Goddess*, p. 155.
3. *Los Angeles Times*, 29 May 1989.
4. Whitmont, *Return of the Goddess*, p. 172.
5. Carol Pearson, *The Hero Within*, p. 125.
6. Sybille Birkhauser-Oeri, *The Mother*, p. 121.
7. Helen Luke, *Woman, Earth and Spirit*, p 63.
8. June Singer, "A Silence of the Soul," p. 32.
9. Erich Neumann, *Amor and Psyche*, p. 140.
10. Ethel Johnston Phelps, *The Maid of the North*.
11. Ibid., p. 37.
12. Ibid., p. 38.
13. Ibid., p. 39.
14. Ibid., p. 40.
15. Ibid., p. 43.
16. Ibid.
17. Ibid., p. 44.
18. Ibid.
19. Whitmont, *Return of the Goddess*, p. 167.
20. Ibid., p. 171.
21. Ibid., p. 173.
22. Bolen, ATP.
23. Betty DeShong Meador, "Uncursing the Dark" pp. 37–38.

24. Janine Canan, ed., *She Rises Like the Sun* (Freedom, Calif: The Crossing Press, 1989), p. 20.

25. Anne Waldman, "Secular/Sexual Musings," p. 13.

Chapter 10. Beyond Duality

1. Martin Buber, *I and Thou*.

2. Thich Nhat Hahn offered a series of retreats and lectures on American Buddhism in the U.S. Excerpts were compiled by Peter Levitt into *The Heart of Understanding*.

3. Ibid.

4. Matthew Fox, *Original Blessing*, p. 54.

5. Interview of Elaine Pagels with Bill Moyers on "World of Ideas."

6. Ibid.

7. Donna Wilshire and Bruce Wilshire, "Gender Stereotypes and Spatial Archetypes."

8. Mary Ann Cejka, "Naming the Sin of Sexism," *Catholic Agitator*, April 1989, p. 2.

9. Wilshire and Wilshire, "Gender Stereotypes," p. 82.

10. *The Early Civilization of Europe*, Monograph for Indo-European Studies 131 (Los Angeles: UCLA, 1980), ch. 2, pp. 32–3, as cited in Riane Eisler, *The Chalice and the Blade*, p. 14.

11. Eisler, *The Chalice and the Blade*, p. 14

12. Ibid.

13. Ibid.

14. Ibid., p. 15.

15. Ibid., p. 18.

16. Ibid., pp. 20–21.

17. Ibid., p. 23–24.

18. Ibid., p. 28.

19. Marija Gimbutas, *Goddesses and Gods of Old Europe, 7000–3500 B.C.*, p. 237.

20. Mircea Eliade, *Patterns in Comparative Religion* 1958, p. 421, as cited in Marta Weigle, *Spiders and Spinsters*, p. 269.

21. Quoted in Weigle, *Spiders and Spinsters*, p. 267.

22. Elaine Pagels, *The Gnostic Gospels*, p. 62.

23. Ibid., p. 64.

24. Ibid., p. 65.

25. Ibid., p. 72.

26. Ibid., pp. 81–82.

27. Edward Whitmont, *Return of the Goddess*, p. 164.

28. Pagels, *The Gnostic Gospels*, p. 82.

29. Author's notes from lectures by Vivienne Hull of the Chinook Community on Iona, Scotland, 20–21 June 1988.

30. José Arguelles and Miriam Arguelles, *Mandala*, p. 23.

31. Ibid., p. 127.
32. Ibid.

Conclusion

1. May Sarton, from "The Invocation to Kali," in Laura Chester and Sharon Barba, eds., *Rising Tides*, p. 67.

Bibliography

BOOKS

Arguelles, José, and Arguelles, Miriam. *Mandala*. Berkeley: Shambhala Publications, 1972.

Birkhauser-Oeri, Sibylle. *The Mother: Archetypal Image in Fairy Tales*. Toronto: Inner City Books, 1988.

Boer, Charles, trans. "The Hymn to Demeter." *Homeric Hymns*. 2nd ed. rev. Texas: Irving, 1979.

Bolen, Jean Shinoda. *Goddesses in Everywoman: A New Psychology of Women*. San Francisco: Harper & Row, 1984.

Buber, Martin. *I and Thou*. New York: Scribner, 1958.

Budapest, Zsuzsanna. *The Holy Book of Women's Mysteries*. Berkeley: Wingbow Press, 1989.

——— *The Grandmother of Time*. San Francisco: Harper & Row, 1989.

Campbell, Joseph. *The Hero with a Thousand Faces*. Bollingen Series 17. Princeton: Princeton University Press, 1949.

———. *The Power of Myth*. New York: Doubleday, 1988.

Canan, Janine, ed. *She Rises Like the Sun*. Freedom, Calif.: The Crossing Press, 1989.

———. *Her Magnificent Body: New and Selected Poems*. Manroot Books, 1986.

Carroll, Lewis. *Alice's Adventures in Wonderland and Through the Looking Glass*. New York: New American Library, 1960.

Chernin, Kim. *Reinventing Eve*. New York: Harper & Row, 1987.

Chester, Laura, and Barba, Sharon, eds. *Rising Tides: 20th Century American Women Poets*, New York: Washington Square Press, 1973.

Christ, Carol P. *Laughter of Aphrodite*. San Francisco: Harper & Row, 1987.

Clift, Jean Dalby, and Clift, Wallace B. *The Hero Journey in Dreams*. New York: Crossroad Publishing Co., 1988.

Dallett, Janet O. *When the Spirits Come Back.* Toronto: Inner City Books, 1988.

Downing, Christine. *The Goddess.* New York: Crossroad Publishing Co., 1981.

Edinger, Edward F. *Ego and Archetype.* New York: Putnam's/Jung Foundation, 1972.

Eisler, Riane. *The Chalice and the Blade.* San Francisco: Harper & Row, 1987.

Fox, Matthew. *Original Blessing.* Santa Fe: Bear & Company, 1983.

Friedan, Betty. *The Second Stage.* New York: Summit Books, 1981.

Gimbutas, Marija. *Goddesses and Gods of Old Europe,* 7000–3500 B.C. Berkeley and Los Angeles: University of California Press, 1982.

Green, Roger L. *Heroes of Greece and Troy.* New York: Walck, 1961.

Griffin, Susan. *Like the Iris of an Eye.* New York: Harper & Row, 1976.

————. *Woman & Nature: The Roaring Inside Her.* New York: Harper & Row, 1978.

Hall, Nor. *The Moon and the Virgin.* New York: Harper & Row, 1980.

Hammer, Signe. *Passionate Attachments: Fathers and Daughters in America Today.* New York: Rawson Associates, 1982.

Hildegard of Bingen. *Illuminations of Hildegard of Bingen.* Commentary by Matthew Fox. Santa Fe: Bear & Company, 1985.

Johnson, Buffie. *Lady of the Beasts.* San Francisco: Harper & Row, 1988.

Johnson, Robert A. *She: Understanding Feminine Psychology.* San Francisco: Harper & Row, 1977.

Jung, Carl Gustav, and Kerenyi, K. "Psychological Aspects of the Kore." *Essays on a Science of Mythology.* New York: Pantheon Books, 1949.

Klein, Mina C., and Klein, H. Arthur, *Käthe Kollwitz: Life in Art.* New York: Schocken Books, 1975.

Kolbenschlag, Madonna. *Kiss Sleeping Beauty Goodbye.* San Francisco: Harper & Row, 1979.

Lauter, Estella. *Woman as Mythmakers: Poetry and Visual Art by Twentieth-Century Women.* Bloomington: Indiana University Press, 1984.

Leonard, Linda Schierse. *The Wounded Woman.* Boston: Shambhala Publications, 1982.

Lerner, Harriet Goldhor. *Women in Therapy.* New York: Harper & Row, 1988.

Levitt, Peter. *The Heart of Understanding.* Berkeley, Calif.: Parallel Press, 1988.

Luke, Helen M. *Woman, Earth and Spirit: The Feminine in Symbol and Myth.* New York: Crossroad Publishing Co., 1981.

Markale, Jean. *Women of the Celts.* Rochester, Vt.: Inner Traditions International, 1986.

Moon, Sheila. *Changing Woman and Her Sisters.* San Francisco: Guild for Psychological Studies, 1984.

Murray, Henry A., ed. *Myth and Mythmaker.* Boston: Beacon Press, 1960.

Neumann, Erich. *Amor and Psyche: The Psychic Development of the Feminine.* Bollingen Series 54. Princeton: Princeton University Press, 1955.

―――. *The Great Mother: An Analysis of the Archetype.* Bollingen Series 47. Princeton: Princeton University Press, 1955.

Pagels, Elaine. *The Gnostic Gospels.* New York: Vintage Books, 1981.

Paris, Ginette. *Pagan Meditations: The Worlds of Aphrodite, Artemis and Hestia.* Dallas: Spring Publications, 1986.

Pearson, Carol. *The Hero Within.* San Francisco: Harper & Row, 1986.

Pearson, Carol, and Pope, Katherine. *The Female Hero in American and British Literature.* New York: R. R. Bowker Co., 1981.

Perera, Sylvia Brinton. *Descent to the Goddess.* Toronto: Inner City Books, 1981.

Phelps, Ethel Johnston. *The Maid of the North: Feminist Folk Tales from Around the World.* New York: Holt, Rinehart, and Winston, 1981.

Rich, Adrienne. *Of Woman Born: Motherhood as Experience and Institution* New York. Bardam Books, 1976.

Sharkey, John. *Celtic Mysteries: The Ancient Religion.* New York: Thames and Hudson, 1975.

Starhawk. *Dreaming the Dark: Magic, Sex and Politics.* Boston: Beacon Press, 1982.

Stone, Merlin. *Ancient Mirrors of Womanhood.* Boston: Beacon Press, 1979.

―――. *When God Was a Woman.* San Diego: Harcourt Brace Jovanovich, 1978.

von Franz, Marie-Louise, and Hillman, James. *Jung's Typology: The Inferior Function and the Feeling Function.* Dallas: Spring Publications, 1971.

Walker, Barbara G. *The Skeptical Feminist.* San Francisco: Harper & Row, 1987.

―――. *The Woman's Encyclopedia of Myths and Secrets.* San Francisco: Harper & Row, 1983.

Weigle, Marta. *Spiders and Spinsters: Women and Mythology.* Albuquerque: University of New Mexico Press, 1982.

Whitmont, Edward C. *Return of the Goddess*. New York: Crossroad Publishing, 1988.

Woodman, Marion. *The Pregnant Virgin: A Process of Psychological Transformation*. Toronto: Inner City Books, 1985.

Wynne, Patrice. *The Womanspirit Sourcebook*. San Francisco: Harper & Row, 1988.

Young-Eisendrath, Polly, and Wiedemann, Florence. *Female Authority: Empowering Women through Psychotherapy*. New York: Guilford Press, 1987.

ARTICLES

Fleming, Patricia C. "Persephone's Search for Her Mother." *Psychological Perspectives*. 15, no. 2 (fall 1984): 127–47.

Jenks, Kathleen. " 'Changing Woman': The Navajo Therapist Goddess." *Psychological Perspectives* 17, no. 2 (fall 1986).

L'Engle, Madeleine. "Shake the Universe." *Ms* magazine. July/August 1987.

Mackay, Kathy. "How Fathers Influence Daughters." *Los Angeles Times*, 6 April 1983.

Meador, Betty DeShong. "Uncursing the Dark: Restoring the Lost Feminine." *Quadrant* 22, no. 1 (1989): 27–39.

Murdock, Maureen. "Changing Women: Contemporary Faces of the Goddess." *Women of Power* 12 (winter 1989).

Rothenberg, Rose-Emily. "The Orphan Archetype." *Psychological Perspectives* 14, no. 2 (fall 1983).

Schmidt, Lynda W. "How the Father's Daughter Found Her Mother." *Psychological Perspectives* 14, no. 1 (spring 1983): 8–19

Singer, June. "A Silence of the Soul: The Sadness of the Successful Woman." *The Quest* (summer 1989).

Travers, P. L. "Out from Eden." *Parabola*, 11, no. 3 (August 1986).

Waldman, Anne. "Secular/Sexual Musings." *Vajradhatu Sun*. 10, no. 6.

Wilshire, Donna W. and Wilshire, Bruce W. "Gender Stereotypes and Spatial Archetypes." *Anima* 15, no. 2 (spring equinox 1989).

POEMS

Connor, Julia. "On the Moon of the Hare." *Making the Good.* Santa Fe: Tooth of Time Books, 1988.

Di Prima, Diane. "Prayer to the Mothers." In Chester, Laura and Barba, Sharon, eds. *Rising Tides*. New York: Washington Square Press, 1973.

Jong, Erica. "Alcestis on the Poetry Circuit." *Half-Live*. New York: Holt, Rinehart & Winston, 1973.

Piercy, Marge. "For Strong Women." In *Circles on the Water: Selected Poems of Marge Piercy*. New York: Alfred A. Knopf, 1982.

Waldman, Anne. "Duality (A Song)." Fast Speaking Music, BMI, 1989.

Credits

Grateful acknowledgment is made to the following poets and their publishers for permission to reprint copyrighted work. Every effort has been made to contact copyright holders.

Janine Canan: "Inanna's Descent," from *Her Magnificent Body, New and Selected Poems* by Janine Canan, © 1986 by Janine Canan, reprinted by permission of Manroot Books.

Julia Connor: "On the Moon of the Hare," from *Making the Good* by Julia Connor, © 1988 (Tooth of Time Press), reprinted with the author's permission.

Diane Di Prima: "Prayer to the Mothers," from *Selected Poems 1956–1975* by Diane Di Prima, © 1976, reprinted with the author's permission. "Ave" from *Loba, Parts 1–8* by Diane Di Prima, © 1978, reprinted with the author's permission.

Susan Griffin: Excerpt from *Like the Iris of an Eye* by Susan Griffin, copyright © 1976 by Susan Griffin. Reprinted by permission of Harper & Row, Publishers, Inc., and the author. Excerpt from *Woman and Nature: The Roaring Inside Her* by Susan Griffin, copyright © 1978 by Susan Griffin. Reprinted by permission of Harper & Row, Publishers, Inc., and the author.

Erica Jong: Excerpt from "Alcestis on the Poetry Circuit," from Half-Lives by Erica Jong. Copyright © 1971, 1972, 1973 by Erica Mann Jong. Reprinted by permission of Henry Holt and Company, Inc.

Rhett Kelly: "Lot's wife" by Rhett Kelly, © 1989 by Rhett Kelly. Reprinted with the author's permission.

Marge Piercy: "For Strong Women" from *Circles on the Water:*

Sources of Illustrations

Index

Books by Maureen Murdock

The Heroine's Journey: Woman's Quest for Wholeness

This book describes contemporary woman's search for wholeness in a society in which she has been defined according to masculine values. Drawing upon cultural myths and fairy tales, ancient symbols and goddesses, and the dreams of contemporary women, Murdock illustrates the need for—and the reality of—feminine values in Western culture today.

Spinning Inward: Using Guided Imagery with Children for Learning, Creativity, and Relaxation

If you have ever wished you could show children and teenagers how to enrich their lives with meditation and visualization, this book will delight you. It presents simple exercises in guided imagery designed to help young people ages three through eighteen to relax into learning, focus attention and increase concentration, stimulate creativity, and cultivate inner peace and group harmony.